Praise for

JOSEPH SMITH'S
21st Century View
OF THE
WORLD

"In addition to being a modern-day Renaissance man (scientist, artist, singer, teacher, writer, and philosopher), John D. Lamb is a latter-day Thomas Aquinas who successfully harmonizes several Restored Gospel truths with the latest scientific discoveries."

—Dr. Madison U. Sowell, Provost, Tusculum University, Greeneville, Tennessee, and past Provost of Southern Virginia University

"I loved this book! In discussing how the gospel insights revealed through Joseph Smith are highly compatible with modern science, it fills a real need in reminding us that rather than being in conflict, religion, and science are more often mutually supportive and fit hand-in-hand as tools for discerning between truth and error. This is a topic we haven't heard discussed so skillfully since the writings of Henry Eyring (an eminent chemist and the father of President Eyring of the First Presidency). The book does a great job of making some fairly complex (and profound!) ideas easily accessible to non-scientists."

—Dr. David V. Dearden, Chair, Department of Chemistry and Biochemistry, Brigham Young University, Provo, Utah

"These concepts provide yet further evidence of Joseph Smith's divine calling. As secrets of the universe are unveiled through science, implicit truths recorded by Joseph Smith reveal God in the details, starting with the smallest of unseen particles that make up this vast universe. The thoughtful study of concepts found in this book reinforce truth as the common denominator uniting science and religion, and offer reassurance to those who may be struggling with perceived conflicts between the two."

—Rick Baird, Salt Lake City, Utah

"In this day and age, we are desperately in need of more material to assist members of the LDS Church, particularly the youth, in the intriguing journey through God's wonders and the scientific method. In this volume, Professor John Lamb does a masterful work in keeping the interest alive as he provides his insights as a Latter-day Saint scientist in reconciling revelations and prophecies recorded by Joseph Smith Jr. with our current understanding of science. The book is exciting, engaging and enlightening. Bravo!"

—Dr. Ugo A. Perego, Visiting Scientist at
the University of Pavia, Italy

"Professor Lamb's well-thought-out explanation of the intersection of recently affirmed science and restored latter-day religion is deeply thought provoking and inspiring. In a logical and entertaining way, John merges both fields of truth into one great whole. This somewhat kaleidoscopic interweaving of science and religion is well documented and leaves the reader with plenty of personal thought starters and just a touch of humor."

—William P. Benac, President, The DFW Alliance
for Religious Freedom, Dallas, Texas

JOSEPH SMITH'S
21st Century View
OF THE
WORLD

⚬⚬ TRUTHS HE KNEW BEFORE ⚬⚬
THE WORLD ACCEPTED THEM

JOHN DAVID LAMB

CFI
An imprint of Cedar Fort, Inc.
Springville, Utah

Scripture quotations taken from the New American Standard Bible® (NASB), Copyright © 1960, 1962, 1963, 1968, 1971, 1972, 1973, 1975, 1977, 1995 by The Lockman Foundation, Used by permission. www.Lockman.org.

ISBN 13: 978-1-4621-2302-5

Published by CFI, an imprint of Cedar Fort, Inc.
2373 W. 700 S., Springville, UT 84663
Distributed by Cedar Fort, Inc., www.cedarfort.com

LIBRARY OF CONGRESS CATALOGING-IN-PUBLICATION DATA

Names: Lamb, John D., author.
Title: Joseph Smith's 21st century view of the world / John David Lamb.
Other titles: Joseph Smith's twenty-first century view of the world
Description: Springville, Utah : CFI, an imprint of Cedar Fort, Inc., [2019]
    | Includes bibliographical references and index.
Identifiers: LCCN 2018052745 (print) | LCCN 2019001074 (ebook) | ISBN
    9781462129997 (epub, pdf, mobi) | ISBN 9781462123025 (perfect bound : alk.
    paper)
Subjects: LCSH: Religion and science. | Physical sciences--Religious
    aspects--Christianity. | Church of Jesus Christ of Latter-day
    Saints--Doctrines. | Mormon Church--Doctrines.
Classification: LCC BX8643.R39 (ebook) | LCC BX8643.R39 L36 2019 (print) |
    DDC 261.5/50882893--dc23
LC record available at https://lccn.loc.gov/2018052745

Cover design by Markie Riley and Jeff Harvey
Cover design © 2019 Cedar Fort, Inc.
Edited by Melissa Caldwell and Misty Moncur
Typeset by Kaitlin Barwick

Printed in the United States of America

10 9 8 7 6 5 4 3 2 1

Printed on acid-free paper

Contents

Preface

In the early years of the nineteenth century in an obscure part of the northwestern wilderness of the newly formed United States of America, a self-proclaimed young prophet was making bold affirmations about God, man, politics, economics, and natural philosophy. These were not subtle variations on past traditions but revolutionary insights and ideas that brought him into conflict with centuries of well-established doctrines in these many areas. His words and works were embraced by some but largely spurned or ignored by the intellectuals of his day. Most of his revelations were theological in nature, but he also revealed much having to do with the earthly prosperity and happiness of God's children and some even about nature itself.

I am speaking, of course, of Joseph Smith. Joseph was anything but a scientist in the academic sense, for his formal education extended only to the third grade. Indeed, his wife Emma, a school teacher herself, made this comment about Joseph's ability to translate the Book of Mormon: "It would have been improbable that a learned man could do this; and for one so ignorant and unlearned as he was, it was simply impossible."[1] Yet in the years following the publication of the Book of Mormon, Joseph produced revelation upon revelation, which exposed uncanny insights into topics well beyond his ken. Included among these were revelations that touch on what we today call science, referring specifically to natural science. Indeed, many of the ideas found among Joseph's insights involved concepts that were either unknown to science in his day or poorly or even wrongly understood. In Joseph's day, his insights drew only derision. But looking back on these claims from the viewpoint of today's science, they were remarkably prescient, and it is clear that Joseph held a very forward-looking, twenty-first-century vision of the world. This is the theme of this book. I will attempt to illuminate specific cases wherein Joseph Smith clearly understood and alluded to scientific principles that came to be accepted and understood only after his death.

Furthermore, I will illustrate just how compatible Joseph's views about the pursuit of truth are with those of modern science. And in doing so, I hope to make a small contribution to the body of work that vindicates his claim as a prophet of God.

Science and religion are often cast as antagonists on the world stage. Joseph did not share this view. He laid claim to any truth from any source, including science, and embraced it wholeheartedly. Indeed, his attitude on this matter may best be summed up in a quote by one of his most ardent followers and companions, Brigham Young, who said:

> The idea that the religion of Christ is one thing, and science is another, is a mistaken idea, for there is no true religion without true science, and consequently there is no true science without true religion.[2]

We live in an era that some have dubbed the *post-truth* era. The implication is that people are no longer interested in what is true or factual but that any opinion is as valid as any other, whether underpinned by reality or not. This is an evil doctrine. Following the lead of Joseph Smith, Latter-day Saints value truth as an eternal principle eagerly to be pursued. We rejoice that additional light and truth have been revealed to mankind in the latter days, thanks to the grace of a loving Heavenly Father. Indeed, Joseph the seer was the possessor and promulgator of truths so sublime that they have inspired generations and will inspire the whole world once they have come to know him.

Over the years, Joseph has had many detractors, resulting in a lively and often heated debate over the validity of individual details found among his writings and teachings, as well as those of his followers. With each criticism and challenge has come a response from Latter-day Saint scholars in the form of a body of apologetic literature—that is, literature providing counterarguments to these objections. This book is not designed to single out and respond to any particular criticisms of Joseph's teachings. Rather, its scope is to illustrate how Joseph possessed a very modern view of the world, one that a twenty-first century person would find fits quite comfortably with what science is now revealing about the world around us.

As this book is not designed to be a science text or a detailed review of the history of science, I have out of necessity simplified many aspects of these otherwise complex and fascinating topics. In doing so, I recognize that experts in these fields may take exception to such generalizations. Readers should be aware that the path of scientific advancement has not been a smooth one, and our current understanding of the world, itself undoubtedly imperfect, has arisen from a series of fits and starts, successes and failures, with ideas coming in and out of vogue, sometimes lost and then rediscovered. But I have attempted to paint as accurate a picture as the broad strokes of my brush would allow, and I encourage those who wish more detail to look to other works, some cited in this book.

In light of President Russell M. Nelson's recent statements, I have made an effort to refer to The Church of Jesus Christ of Latter-day Saints, its members, and its teachings using proper terminology. To avoid frequent repetition of the full name, I have used "restored Church of Jesus Christ" or simply the capitalized word "Church" to refer to this church in particular throughout the work.

My sincere thanks to those who have offered helpful insights into this writing: my wife, Betty; my son, Jeremy; my current and former BYU colleagues David Dearden and Madison Sowell; and my good friends Rick Baird and Ugo Perego. Furthermore, I owe special gratitude to my wife, Betty, for her unfailing support over many years of her eccentric husband.

NOTES

1. "Last Testimony of Sister Emma," *Saints' Herald*, **26** (Oct. 1879), p. 290.
2. *Journal of Discourses*, Albert Carrington Pub., Liverpool, 1875, **17**, p. 52; Brigham Young discourse, 3 May 1874.

Chapter 1

JOSEPH SMITH AND LATTER-DAY SCIENCE

Could you gaze into heaven five minutes, you would know more than you would by reading all that ever was written on the subject. (Joseph Smith, Nauvoo, Illinois, October 9, 1843, History of the Church, **6**, *p. 50)*

On a chilly Sunday afternoon in the early spring of 1836, the strains of a new Latter-day Saint hymn cascaded down from a wooded plateau into the beautiful Chagrin Valley just south of Lake Erie in the state of Ohio. About a thousand voices strong, this congregation was electrified with excitement, and it showed in the enthusiasm with which they sang. Their prophet had just read a lengthy prayer of dedication, received earlier by revelation, invoking the blessings of God on their new temple and on this young flock of converts who had sacrificed so much in money and toil over the last three years to build it. The edifice itself was something of a miracle, an echo of New England church architecture with significant customization to meet the demands of a new and unique theology. The finished work was a wonder to behold, and no doubt the celebrants on that day took pride in whatever architectural embellishment each singer could point to as his or her small contribution. They marveled that in their poverty they could erect such a glorious space in which to worship, the estimated $50,000 cost beyond any sum that most of them could even imagine. As they had entered hours earlier, they could read the plaque above the heavy green doors denoting this edifice as the "House of the Lord." They had sat enthralled in their new

1

temple for hours on that day, oblivious of the hard, wooden benches and the cheek-to-jowl accommodations, for it was standing room only at the dedication of the Kirtland temple.[1]

The song the Saints were singing on that day was introduced by the prophet Joseph Smith as "Hosanah [sic] to God and the Lamb," the last entry in the newly printed hymnbook of the fledgling Church. Many in the congregation had their copies, tiny (3 x 4.5 inch) pocket-friendly editions containing ninety hymns chosen by the prophet's wife Emma—words only, no notes, no harmonies, no treble clefs. Others may have found the words provided on white satin as the prophet had ordered for the occasion. Today, we know the hymn as "The Spirit of God," and it is still sung with the same spirit and enthusiasm as on that first rendition in March 1836, although not necessarily to the same tune. It is believed that it was first voiced to the tune Latter-day Saint congregations sing today to "Now Let Us Rejoice." But in fact, it is the words, not the music, of the hymn that inform our discussion here, and for these we owe a debt of gratitude to an early Latter-day Saint leader of some poetic genius.

William Wines Phelps had joined the Latter-day Saint faith not long after its organization in 1830, and he contributed much to fulfill its publication needs. He authored the words to more than a dozen early Church hymns, including the one described here, as well as other familiar hymns, such as "Redeemer of Israel," "Praise to the Man," and "If You Could Hie to Kolob." Before his conversion, he had served as the prominent New York editor of several newspapers. After accepting the new faith, he served as the Church printer and editor in Jackson County, Missouri, before being physically assaulted along with his family and ejected from that region with all the Saints in 1833. His association with the Church ran into a few snags over subsequent years, as seems commonplace among early prominent brethren, but he died in full fellowship in Salt Lake City in 1872, having contributed much over many years to the building of the kingdom.

Among the inspired phrases of Phelps's hymn sung on the occasion of the Kirtland temple dedication are words that reflect the strong influence of the latter-day prophet under whose tutelage he worked. We find these words in the Church's current hymnbook, on page 2: "The Lord is extending the Saints' understanding. . . . The veil o'er the earth is beginning to burst." It is likely that neither he nor any of those singing those words in March 1836 on that solemn occasion, perhaps with the exception of Brother Joseph himself, could have appreciated the magnitude of that claim so boldly expressed in song. It is only now in retrospect that we can begin to fathom the meaning of those prophetic words, for in very fact the scale of the universe, which is now opening up to us as a result of scientific inquiry, is truly breathtaking, both on the extremes of the very large and the very small. As a scientist, I am struck by how true the words of the song have been manifest. Indeed, it is as if, until the recent historical past, our sight had been hindered by a covering of darkness, a veil, and that gradually over the last few hundred years that veil has begun to melt away, like the fog retreating before the coming of the dawn. Knowledge concerning God's creations is pushing back the darkness in these latter days.

On numerous occasions, the prophet Joseph made it clear in his revelations that knowledge was a central power through which God's designs for the latter days would be achieved. A poignant episode later in the prophet's life illustrates this point quite markedly. While enduring the misery of a cold, dark, comfortless jail cell in Liberty, Missouri, in winter of 1839, Joseph asked in great anguish, "Oh God, where art thou?" (D&C 121:1) Perhaps you know the story—the Saints had been driven from their homes, indeed from the whole state of Missouri in the cold of winter, and the whole Church had been brought down to near destruction. Joseph and others had spent the entire winter in an unheated, unfurnished dungeon. In answer to Joseph's plea, what comfort did the Lord have to offer? If we turn to Doctrine and Covenants 121, we find the answer:

- First, the Lord invokes the immensity of time—"thine afflictions shall be but a small moment," he says, and the hope of the enemies of the Saints "shall be blasted." (verses 7 and 11)
- Second, he comforts Joseph and the Saints with promises of great knowledge. (verses 26–33)
- Third, he gives promises and exhortations regarding priesthood. (verses 34–46)

While we usually focus our attention on this last topic, notice that a significant part of the comfort the Lord offers is to be derived from knowledge. He offers up these promises:

All thrones and dominions, principalities and powers, shall be revealed and set forth upon all who have endured valiantly for the gospel of Jesus Christ. And also, if there be bounds set to the heavens or to the seas, or to the dry land, or to the sun, moon, or stars—All the times of their revolutions, all the appointed days, months, and years, and all the days of their days, months, and years, and all their glories, laws, and set times, shall be revealed in the days of the dispensation of the fulness of times— . . . How long can rolling waters remain impure? What power shall stay the heavens? As well might man stretch forth his puny arm to stop the Missouri river in its decreed course, or to turn it up stream, as to hinder the Almighty from pouring down knowledge from heaven upon the heads of the Latter-day Saints. (D&C 121:29–31, 33)

Can knowledge really be a source of comfort? What value and comfort do we find as Latter-day Saints in knowledge? Surely, we'd all agree that knowledge of the gospel itself can comfort and inspire. But can so-called secular knowledge do so as well? When you stop and think about it, it should—that is, when you consider that all truth comes from God. He doesn't make the distinction between sacred and secular truth—to him it is all one; it is all truth. In this work, as we pursue various topics together, I trust that you will find examples wherein both sacred and secular knowledge can be both a comfort and inspiration to you as it has been to me.

The coming forth of gospel truth in the latter days has been paralleled by an explosion of scientific truth. In certain respects, these two fields of knowledge have found harmony since Joseph Smith's time in ways that only now are we coming to appreciate. This is the underlying theme of this work. It has been motivated in part by my personal concern that too often we tend to dwell on areas where science and religion appear to conflict. And this has been a source of consternation and a test of faith for many. I say "appear to conflict" because in fact we must recognize that there can be only one truth, and where science and religion intersect and overlap in their claims, those who value both as reliable sources can rightly expect them to harmonize. Herein I will endeavor to provide a few examples where, in recent times, past areas of apparent conflict have been wondrously resolved, so that where once there was disharmony, a new harmony has arisen. And thereby we may entertain hope and faith that where apparent conflicts remain, with the gathering of new knowledge in both science and theology, those seeming discontinuities will be resolved like the ones that have already found resolution.

The reader may in fairness ask where my personal bias lies, given that I am both a practicing member of The Church of Jesus Christ of Latter-day Saints and a scientist. By nature, I have always been curious to get to the heart of understanding in all areas of knowledge—hence my proclivity toward a scientific career since childhood. The Latin root of the word *science* is *knowledge*, and it is only in the last couple of hundred years that science has taken on the connotation of what we can more strictly term *natural science*, embracing fields like chemistry, physics, biology, and so on. I think of myself as a scientist in the broader sense of the word and look for true knowledge wherever I can find it. This attitude echoes that of the most famous of Latter-day Saint chemists, Henry Eyring: "Here is the spirit of true religion, an honest seeking after knowledge of all things of heaven and earth."[2] Indeed, a valuing of knowledge as a fundamental aspect of Latter-day Saint theology goes right back to the very roots of the restoration, when the prophet Joseph remarked, "In knowledge there is power. God has more power than all other beings, because he has greater knowledge . . ."[3]

We are blessed to live in a day when knowledge is expanding, and the veil of darkness which obscured our vision of the true nature of the world and our place in it for so many centuries is being lifted. As this process unfolds, new insights in both science and theology resolve old questions in some cases and raise new questions in others. In this work we shall explore some of these questions together, and in the process, seek faith that in the end, knowledge derived from both areas of understanding will find perfect harmony under one complete framework of truth. In particular, we shall see that on several key points, Joseph Smith was remarkably prescient in his understanding of the natural world, anticipating the science that we have now come to understand in the twenty-first century.

Notes

1. Details about the construction and dedicatory services of the Kirtland temple may be found in Elwin C. Robison, *The First Mormon Temple*, Brigham Young University Press, 1997.

2. Henry Eyring, *Reflections of a Scientist*, Deseret Book, 1983, p. 3.

3. Joseph Fielding Smith, *Teachings of the Prophet Joseph Smith*, Deseret Book, 1973, p. 288. More fully documented collections of Joseph's teachings are available in two more recent sources: the volume prepared by Andrew F. Ehat and Lyndon W. Cook, *The Words of Joseph Smith*, Religious Studies Monograph Series, Religious Studies Center, Brigham Young University, 1980; and *The Joseph Smith Papers*, available online at https://josephsmithpapers.org.

Chapter 2

THE WORLD WE THOUGHT WE KNEW

Lift up your eyes on high And see who has created these stars, The One who leads forth their host by number, He calls them all by name; Because of the greatness of His might and the strength of His power, Not one of them is missing. (Isaiah 40:26)[1]

Have you ever been tempted to count the stars in the sky? I suppose if you looked up into the moonless sky on a cloudless night in downtown Los Angeles or Beijing, that might not seem such a hopeless task—the pollution would allow you to see only a few dozen stars. But if you were to go out into the countryside and look up, that would be a different matter altogether! Our family experienced that difference when we often went to camp in southern Utah—a favorite pastime at night was to stare up into the clear night sky together and share the wonder of what seemed an unfathomable number of stars. No one was tempted to count them one by one—that would take all night, and you would doubtless lose track or fall asleep halfway through. But it was fun to try to identify individual stars and constellations, as I suppose countless humans have done over the ages.

In fact, people have always been fascinated by the stars. Looking back in history, the study of the stars and planets was one of the first serious endeavors in what we today call science, an attempt to make sense of the natural world around us. It is no surprise that the heavens would serve this pioneering role, as they are readily observable with the naked eye (especially in years gone by when skies were free of pollution and nighttime lighting), and they follow a regular and reliable pattern of behavior. Not only that, but the patterns of behavior of the heavenly bodies have real practical significance—they parallel the patterns of our climate and therefore can be used to predict and plan for times of warmth and cold, rain and drought, and thus the migrations of prey animals and the proper planting and harvesting of crops.

We take for granted today that we know at every moment where in the climate cycle we stand, but this was not the case hundreds and thousands of years ago, when there were no calendars on the walls, no watches or cell phones to tell us what day it was or what time it was. Even today, though we don't individually have to sync our wristwatches with the movements of the sun, moon, and stars, somebody must do this, and we rely on experts to find these things out for us and send them along invisibly to our devices. Thus it has been from time immemorial. Thousands of years ago, farmers did not prognosticate by the stars—that was left to the experts of the day, not called scientists, but priests and wise men, the specialists of yesteryear.

Given the long-standing connection between religion and astronomy, let's begin our discussion of today's science and Joseph Smith's theology by focusing our attention on the heavens. But first a little history. Indeed, we cannot fully appreciate the revolutionary nature of Joseph's teachings without a clear backdrop against which these new teachings emerged. This will take the form of a brief summary of the historical development of modern science and its relationship with religion in general.[2] To do so, we start with the Greeks. While it is likely that they inherited much of their understanding from earlier civilizations, the roots going back to the biblical patriarchs, reliable records concerning the development of modern science begin there, with the Greeks.

As mentioned, the first serious attempts to understand the natural world focused on the heavens, as observed with the naked eye. Over time, ancient astronomers collected a lot of information about the times, positions, and motions of the sun, moon, stars, and planets (what today scientists call *data*). And with sufficient data, they were then able to start developing models to describe how the heavens were constructed. The Greeks excelled at this effort, and over time there were principally two competing models championed by two sets of Greek philosophers anciently:

- The so-called pre-Socratic philosophers (those who lived before Socrates) taught that each star was a sun, with worlds of its own. To them, these were material worlds like our own, which behaved by the same principles as objects on earth. One such philosopher was Democritus, who lived around 400 BC and who also held to political principles similar to those of modern-day democracies (note the name). His model, which was entirely secular and did not include the influence of gods on the world, lost the competition for popular acceptance to the following model which came along a little later.

- Aristotle and his compatriots, who lived around 350 BC, devised an elaborate model of the *world*, which we call the *universe*, with the earth at the center and the planets (including the sun and the moon) and the stars circling it. An important aspect of this model was the idea that objects on the earth obey one set of physical laws, while everything else from the moon outward obeys an entirely different set of laws. To Aristotle, earthly objects are material and heavy; heavenly objects are not—they are *ethereal*. For example, earthly objects naturally fall down toward the center of the *world*, not because there exists anything like a force of gravity, but because that's just what earthly objects do—they naturally fall to the center of the universe. By contrast, the natural motion of heavenly objects is to move in perfect circles around the center of the world, for no other reason than that's what heavenly objects do by their very nature. Everything on the earth, including intelligent beings (people), is considered mortal, fallible, corrupt; everything in the heavens, including intelligent beings (gods), is perfect, unchanging, eternal. The stars are not suns; there is only one planetary system, our own, with the earth at the center, or better said, at the *bottom* of the universe.

Note that the pre-Socratic model was more in line with the model we subscribe to today. But I've described the Aristotelian model in greater detail for an important reason. Though it was developed long before the advent of Christianity, it was adopted early on by the Christian church after the great apostasy and eventually became accepted as near doctrine. As such, it ran into conflict with emerging modern science in the sixteenth and following centuries, and so will be an important subject for our discussion of the interface between science and religion.

Indeed, the conflict between the two Greek models I've described had a certain aspect of science versus religion even in the fourth-century-BC Greek world. The pre-Socratic model, which described the whole universe as being earth-like, held no place for the Greek gods, like Zeus and Apollo, and so did not fit with the commonly held view that individual gods governed the behavior of volcanoes, earthquakes, rivers, trees, animals, and everything. This pre-Socratic model was so foreign to the prevailing religious culture that it was easily supplanted by the Aristotelian model that had a place for the gods—namely the heavens. The Aristotelian model even allowed for the planets in the heavens to represent individual gods. Keep in mind that for the Greeks, there were seven planets: the sun, the moon, Mercury, Venus, Mars, Jupiter, and Saturn. They were called *planets* because the root of the word means *wanderers*, given that from night to night, these bright lights moved to a different spot in the sky against the background of the fixed stars, which did not move from night to night relative to one another. And, of course, these planets all revolved around the center of the universe, which was a point located at the center of the earth, where the dirt and refuse of the universe had fallen and collected to form the earth itself.

The Aristotelian model was adopted by Christianity for many of the same reasons it appealed to the ancient Greeks. Foremost, it held a place in its structure for the existence of deity. Christian doctrine taught that the earth and its inhabitants were in a fallen state, mortal, fallible, corrupt, just like the Aristotelian model. The model provided a place for the Christian God and angels to reside, that is, the heavens, which were perfect and unchanging. Furthermore, this model and its slight variations were pretty good at describing and predicting the actual paths of the motion of the planets, and therefore were of practical use in keeping the calendar, which was one of the responsibilities of the Church. It was Saint Thomas Aquinas in thirteenth-century Italy who made a convincing case that this model was so excellent that it should be adopted formally by the Roman Catholic Church. Indeed, until much more accurate data about planetary motions became available, it satisfied pretty much everybody, from astronomers to priests, and so held strong popular sway for nearly two thousand years. As such, it wins the longevity prize for scientific models, although not the validity prize.

The man who is held largely responsible for upsetting this pleasant state of affairs is the Polish cleric Mikolaj Kopernik, a.k.a. Nicolaus Copernicus. Around AD 1500, with new data at hand, Nicolaus had the audacity to show that from a mathematical point of view, it was just as valid, and less complicated, to model the world with the sun at the center, rather than the earth. Furthermore, Copernicus was not the only radical thinker around that time; indeed, some were dreaming even *more* radical ideas. One such was Giordano Bruno, an Italian monk who resurrected the idea that the stars were distant suns in a possibly infinite universe, each with its own planets (sound familiar?). He even postulated that some planets might have life, and perhaps even people, aboard. For his trouble, and for other crimes, such as questioning Christ's divinity, Bruno was burned at the stake in AD 1600 in Rome. By contrast, Copernicus avoided the fate of heretics by failing to insist that his model was more than a mathematical nicety.

Decades after Copernicus published his ideas, more serious problems for the Aristotelian model arose when in Italy Galileo Galilei pointed his new telescope at the heavens in 1609. His observations provided actual physical proofs that the Aristotelian model was seriously flawed. He saw moons circling Jupiter, which should not have been there; he saw mountains on the moon, which should not have been there; he saw that Venus showed phases like the moon (full Venus, crescent Venus, and so forth), which should not have been there. Why should these things not have been there? Because according to Aristotle, the heavens were supposed to be perfect, smooth, without blemish, unchanging, and centered on the earth. Yet Galileo showed that the only way to describe these observations was in terms of a sun-centered, rather than an earth-centered, *solar system*. To add to these troubles, others had shown that the planets were moving about the sun in oval (elliptical) orbits, rather than the perfect circles that the Aristotelian model required. The adopted pact between Aristotelian natural philosophy and orthodox religion (both Catholic and Protestant) was broken, resulting in a serious crisis. Galileo became a victim of the resulting tensions and spent the last several years of his life under Inquisition house arrest for these beliefs. He was lucky to escape with his life.

The transition from the Aristotelian model to the modern model of the solar system (the universe that you studied in school) culminated with the work of Isaac Newton in England in the late seventeenth century. Newton is famous for the law of gravitation, and, indeed, that insight constituted a stroke of genius. But for our story here, his most important contribution is this: he proved once and for all that the same laws govern objects on the earth and in the heavens. I think you can see how this drives the last nail into the coffin of the Aristotelian model, which is constructed on the foundation that objects in the heavens obey different laws than do objects on the earth.

How did Newton accomplish this? Let's revisit the apocryphal tale of Newton and the apple. Newton is sitting under an apple tree, and an apple falls on his head. He is so stunned by this event that he instantly invents the law of gravity—right? Wrong. Here's the more accurate version: Newton sees an apple fall to the ground, and then he looks up and sees the moon high above, slowly circling the Earth. He has an aha moment. What if the motion of the two objects is really alike, the only difference being that, unlike the apple, the moon is also moving sideways as it falls to the earth? In fact, Newton envisions that the moon is moving sideways so fast, that as it falls, the earth curves away under it, and it never reaches the surface of the earth. It just continues falling forever while keeping its sideways motion. It is in orbit.

Thereafter, Newton showed in detailed terms that what made the apple fall to the ground (*gravity*) was the same phenomenon (the *force of gravity*) that made the moon go around the earth. And in fact, he also showed that this was the same force that made the earth and the other planets go around the sun, and so on. What really clinched his argument was the precision with which this model could describe and predict the motions of such bodies, not just in descriptive terms, but mathematically to within very exacting measurements. In other words, his model described the motions of things both on the earth and in the heavens to an amazingly accurate degree using one and the same set of laws. The motion of the apple and the moon could be described using the same equations. Indeed, Newton's model has stood the test of time so well that the same three-hundred-year-old equations were used to send men to the moon and back safely, and to send spacecraft far afield of the earth to this day. Newton is most commonly remembered as the discoverer of the law of gravity, but although this was an amazing insight in itself, its influence on the development of modern science pales in comparison to his establishing once and for all that the laws of nature are universal, applying both on the earth and in the heavens.

These developments revolutionized human understanding of the nature of the world and seriously upset the sense of harmony between science (called *natural philosophy* in Newton's day) and religion, which had prevailed for thousands of years. Before that time, there had been one harmonious *truth* common to both fields, at least since the time of Aquinas. Now people had to try to rationalize two apparently conflicting bodies of truth, as what was taught by religion seemed increasingly out of step with what was taught by science. Thus, the gradual demise of the church-anointed Aristotelian model led to a building crisis of faith among Christians. If religion could be so wrong for so long in staunchly defending Aristotle, what else might it be wrong about? And beyond this, there arose an even more fundamental problem: Newton's model so accurately depicted the universe as a well-tuned machine that people started wondering if they had any need for God at all. Maybe the universe was just a mindless machine of which each person was just one of many moving parts.

For some, science was becoming a replacement for religion. If we could but find out all of nature's rules by which she operated, we could predict and describe everything we saw without the need for invoking a god of nature at all. Who needs an all-powerful god if everything runs by itself?

This crisis of faith laid the groundwork for much soul-searching and re-evaluating of long-held beliefs among Christians. To be thorough, these events did not occur in a vacuum but were paralleled by other social and religious pressures associated with the Reformation and the Enlightenment. But this is not a history book, and I have outlined this scientific history solely to set the stage for a discussion of Joseph Smith's revolutionary claims about the nature of God and of his creations. For neither does Joseph's story occur in a vacuum.

As mentioned in the previous chapter, through the harsh winter of 1838–39, Joseph Smith and other Church leaders were held in a cold, comfortless dungeon in Missouri. In despair, Joseph cried out to the Lord for comfort as recorded in Doctrine and Covenants 121. In response, the Lord offered Joseph solace in the form of knowledge of the heavens, the seas, the dry land, the sun, moon, and stars. With this history in mind, we will see the hand of the Lord in preparing the world for new truths to come to light in these the latter days. And with this knowledge comes comfort not only to Joseph and his contemporaries but to modern Saints as well. This comfort comes in a rather unique way—the validation of modern revelation concerning mankind and its relationship to deity as affirmed by a new harmony between what is taught in latter-day scripture and what science has uncovered about the world since the time of that scripture's revealing, as discussed in the next and subsequent chapters.

NOTES

1. Scripture quotation taken from the New American Standard Bible® (NASB), Copyright © 1960, 1962, 1963, 1968, 1971, 1972, 1973, 1975, 1977, 1995 by The Lockman Foundation, Used by permission. www. Lockman.org.

2. A detailed account of the history of science may be found in Stephen F. Mason's book *A History of the Sciences*, Macmillan General Reference, 1962; a less detailed, popularized account is found in Bill Bryson's book *A Short History of Nearly Everything*, Broadway Books, 2004.

Chapter 3

GOD'S UNIVERSE REVEALED

The heavens declare the glory of God; and the firmament sheweth his handywork. (Psalm 19:1)

In your trips to the wild parts of the world, you have probably seen that beautiful band of stars stretching from one horizon to the other called the Milky Way. Only a few ancient philosophers thought that it consisted of distant stars; most considered it a phenomenon of the upper atmosphere. Yet, at the same time that Newton was revealing a mechanical model of objects both on the earth and in the heavens, scientific technology was advancing steadily and resolving questions like the true nature of the Milky Way. For example, the telescope that Galileo used to revolutionize human thought about the world was really no better or bigger than a youngster's science fair telescope of today. Later, in the years before Joseph Smith's birth, much larger telescopes were being used to show that there are many more stars than can be seen with the naked eye, and it was made clear that the Milky Way was really a band of distant stars. The idea was floated that the universe consisted of a swirl of stars, which we see as the Milky Way. This swirl was given the title *island universe*. Today, we think of the Milky Way as one of many *galaxies* (a Greek term for milky way), but in the early nineteenth century, the galaxy we live in was considered by most observers to be the only one—that was the whole universe, consisting of a large but finite number of stars.

This was the status of human understanding of the universe among scholars in Joseph Smith's day. However, it is unclear how many of these new ideas had made their way into the wilds of western New York state,

Ohio, or Missouri. What *is* clear is that the promise made by the Lord to Joseph in Liberty Jail, that during the term of this dispensation much would be revealed about the universe, has indeed come to pass. Let's consider what humankind has learned on this subject since the gospel restoration began.

First, how many stars do scientists say that there are? If you ask your local astronomer how many stars you can see with the naked eye, she'll tell you it's about ten thousand on the best of nights. The answer will vary a little depending on whom you ask, but it will be in that ballpark. And for thousands of years, that's how many stars it seemed there were. But in the last couple of hundred years, we've begun to realize that there are a lot more than ten thousand. And just as the Lord has promised, in the dispensation of the fulness of times, new knowledge about our universe has been accumulating at a breathtaking and accelerating rate.

Probably the most recent and dramatic contribution to our understanding of the real scope of the universe results from the launching and subsequent fixing of the Hubble space telescope. That telescope is named after the early-twentieth-century astronomer who first discovered with his ground-based telescope that certain little smudges of light seen with earlier, smaller telescopes were not clouds in our Milky Way but were in fact other galaxies outside our own. It is therefore perfectly fitting that his namesake modern-day space telescope would discover something even more amazing about galaxies—that there are billions, perhaps trillions of them!

One especially amazing experiment done with the Hubble space telescope is worth special attention. Astronomers noticed a tiny patch of sky that seemed to have no stars or galaxies even at the highest magnification. Since they were using a camera, they were able to do what photographers often do in dim light—they figuratively left the lens cap off to take a long exposure. They pointed the telescope at that one patch of seemingly empty sky for ten days to collect all the light they could. And what did they see? To their amazement, they found this apparently empty bit of space to be full of galaxies so far away that their light was too dim to see otherwise. It seemed that there were galaxies everywhere, even in places that seemed empty of anything.

So what's the answer to our question? How many stars are there? Well, brace yourself, because the answer is truly awe-inspiring. Again, depending on whom you ask, you'll get an answer something like this:

there are about 200 billion stars in the Milky Way Galaxy, and there are between 100 and 1000 billion galaxies in the known universe!

Now that answer merits some serious pondering.

Unfortunately, we've become rather glib about using big numbers nowadays—with national debts in the trillions and gigabytes in our computers, these numbers roll easily off the tongue, but what do they mean? Even on the surface, you can tell we're talking about a lot of stars. But it is difficult to really appreciate how big these numbers are. The difficulty reminds me of some verses in revealed latter-day scripture that also speak of the immense number of worlds in the cosmos.

First, let's turn to Enoch, who is shown the cosmos by the Lord and says:

> And were it possible that man could number the particles of the earth, yea, millions of earths like this, it would not be a beginning to the number of thy creations; and thy curtains are stretched out still. (Moses 7:30)

And now to Abraham:

> Thus I, Abraham, talked with the Lord, face to face, as one man talketh with another; and he told me of the works which his hands had made; And he said unto me: My son, my son (and his hand was stretched out), behold I will show you all these. And he put his hand upon mine eyes, and I saw those things which his hands had made, which were many; and they multiplied before mine eyes, and I could not see the end thereof. (Abraham 3:11–12)

And now to Moses:

> And he [Moses] beheld also the inhabitants thereof, and there was not a soul which he beheld not; and he discerned them by the Spirit of God; and their numbers were great, even numberless as the sand upon the sea shore. And he beheld many lands; and each land was called earth, and there were inhabitants on the face thereof. (Moses 1:28–29)

It's interesting that repeatedly in the revelations, when the Lord is trying to help us imagine huge numbers of things, he alludes to the grains of sand on the beach. And there's another reason this metaphor is especially fascinating to a scientist: because it pops up in another, entirely unrelated place. In his television series *Cosmos*, a scientist who is not a believer in God, Carl Sagan, tries to help the viewer understand the enormous numbers of stars that modern science has revealed through instruments like the Hubble telescope. Lo and behold, he states that the number of stars in the known universe is greater than the number of grains of sand on all the beaches of the planet earth.[1] Now, when I first heard that, I must admit I did a double take—as a scientist, I tend to be skeptical of hyperbolic claims. I wanted to check this out for myself, so I did my own calculations using outlandish estimates of the amount of beach property on earth, the average depth of sand on a beach, and so on. That's something you can try for yourself—and if you do you'll be astonished to find that Carl's about right.

Imagine how many stars that represents! Imagine standing on a huge beach, the sand stretching out for miles before you. Reach down and gather up a handful of sand and imagine trying to count the number of grains just in your hand. Now imagine all the sand on all the beaches. Since Carl made that claim, we have come to understand that in addition to the sand on the beaches, you can add in all the grains of sand on all the deserts as well—including the Sahara, the Gobi, the Arabian, all of them. That's how many stars there are!

Here's another way to help us put these big numbers in perspective: Let's pretend you are the captain of the starship Enterprise, and you have set out to explore the universe, to go where no one has gone before. You wish to identify all the inhabited solar systems in the universe, and so you set out. But you have an important advantage over these TV captain explorers. You have a new super-charged Enterprise that can ignore all the effects of relativity and acceleration (so long, Einstein!) and get from one star to another in one second. You then have one second to explore that solar system and move on to the next. You begin your exploration the second you are born (you are a very precocious child!) and you continue it non-stop for your one-hundred-year life span. You don't stop for lunch, or to sleep, or to open your Christmas presents. How many stars will you have visited at the end of your journey? It turns out only about 1.5 billion.

How discouraging! You worked really hard, but you've only managed to visit less than 1 percent of the stars in our own galaxy, let alone any of the other 100 billion to 1,000 billion galaxies out there. So, how long would it take to visit all the stars at this rate? About 10 trillion years! Wow, I think I'd get tired and give up long before that.

Clearly, we need a plan B. Maybe we could limit the number of stars we need to visit to just those that have planets. Would that significantly cut back on the time required? Until just about a decade ago, we couldn't answer that question, but now we can. New technologies have made it possible to look for planets around other stars. And guess what—there are planets around nearly all of them, with several thousand planets discovered by the date of this writing in 2018. And to narrow the search further, what if we were to limit our search only to planets that orbit their stars in just the right place that they might have liquid water and, therefore, life. Researchers now estimate that billions of stars in our own galaxy have not just any planets, but planets in the so-called habitable zone capable of supporting life. Even with these added restrictions, we wouldn't be able to visit all the planets of interest in our one galaxy in a lifetime travelling constantly this way, let alone any of the other galaxies.

These are really awesome thoughts! Do they inspire you? They do me. And maybe they help take your mind off your personal problems a bit and put them into perspective. Is this comforting? Perhaps this is why the Lord offered such knowledge to Joseph Smith in Liberty Jail as a source of comfort.

I have to admit that when faced with the scope of the universe, a person might have a different response than the one I've alluded to above. Rather than inspiring, one might find it extremely depressing to think that we are so insignificant—tiny living organisms on a tiny insignificant planet among trillions in the universe. But that is where knowledge of and faith in a living God makes all the difference. If we are the very offspring of him who created and is master of all this magnificence, and if we indeed stand to inherit "all that [our] Father hath," (D&C 84:38) what greater hope and inspiration could we have?

Not only can thinking about the scope of the universe as revealed both in modern scripture and by modern science take our minds off our problems, or at least put them in perspective, but it also can help us see our true place in the universe. We are not just like insignificant ants in an endless landscape; we are potential heirs to the King of all we see around us. How inspiring!

Remember the words of the hymn *How Great thou Art*? "O Lord my God, when I, in awesome wonder, consider all the worlds thy hands have made, . . . then sings my soul." (*Hymns*, no. 86) As you can imagine, it's hard to be discouraged when your soul is singing. It's hard to look at the night sky and think of the scale of the universe and be depressed if you understand your true place in the scheme of things. What Joseph Smith came to understand as he was taught by the Lord and what mankind has learned about the stars through science has become a source of both comfort and inspiration available to all God's children. And chances are you'll never look at the night sky again without thinking about these ideas.

I believe that no thinking human being can come up against these newly revealed truths without feeling a sense of awe at the vastness and complexity of our universe. For us, as Latter-day Saints, this kind of insight comprises a striking testimony of the greatness of God's power. Others, like Carl Sagan, feel the awe and wonder but are not convinced that God is behind it all. One might ask, why the difference? In part, it is because we as Latter-day Saints do not derive our testimonies from nature's wonders, but our testimonies come from the voice of the Spirit to our hearts. Having received the witness, though, the awe we feel at nature's wonders finds a comfortable home in our testimonies, it reinforces faith, it confirms and enlarges what we already know to be true. And keeping this kind of perspective inspires us and helps us to endure the challenges of life—yes, sometimes great suffering—just as Joseph was able to endure in Liberty Jail.

When we look at the night sky, and in many other ways, the wonders of nature bear witness to us day in and day out of a Heavenly Father who brings order to all we see around us. Ask yourself: How often do I stop to listen to these witnesses? If you're like me, the answer is "not often enough." That's unfortunate because every time we do, we are healed to some degree of life's wounds. Every time we do, we grow in appreciation of God's great plan in which all of nature participates. It heartens me to know that I, together with you, lie at the center of that plan. Just think that all this vast creation was made for you and me! Doesn't that make you feel both humble and wonderful at the same time?

A significant lesson can be learned from this story. It is rather astonishing to think that Joseph Smith understood the scope of the universe in the early 1800s well before science had revealed it. Just before his time, scientists like Kant and Herschel in Europe and Benjamin Franklin in America had been speculating about the existence of multiple worlds.

But Joseph went further, and in his works of revelation, referring to the writings of Moses and Abraham cited above, and in the Doctrine and Covenants, he made claims about the number of stars and planets that were outlandish and unsubstantiated in his day, and which held him up for possible ridicule and eventual discrediting. He even claimed that there were countless inhabited planets, an outrageous proposition for the science of his day, but one which is now considered a serious possibility by respected scientists. Why would Joseph risk criticism unnecessarily like this if he were inventing these things? In the intervening years, he has been vindicated by science, and this stands as a significant witness to his prophetic calling. Whereas in his day there was an apparent conflict between the claims of his theology and those of science concerning the scope of the universe and the proliferation of worlds, in the intervening years, this conflict has been resolved as science has broadened its understanding. And it has been resolved in favor of revealed truth, much to the astonishment of many.

Today there are other apparent disconnects between Joseph's theology and science, and these have been a stumbling block to some. Perhaps we can learn a lesson from this particular instance. Where we may encounter other apparent conflicts between science and religion today, we can have faith that as further light and knowledge are gained in both the areas of theology and science, these apparent conflicts will be resolved, and that a common truth will be found in the end. After all, both science and religion share in the common quest for truth, and all truth centers in him who calls himself by that name.

NOTE

1. Carl Sagan, *Cosmos*, Digitally Remastered Disc Collector's Edition, Cosmos Studios Inc., 2000.

Chapter 4

WHAT THE EYE CAN'T SEE

For by my Spirit will I enlighten them, and by my power will I make known unto them the secrets of my will—yea, even those things which eye has not seen, nor ear heard, nor yet entered into the heart of man. (D&C 76:10)

This morning I was admiring pictures on my computer screen of faraway galaxies taken by the Hubble space telescope—breathtaking vistas of stars, galaxies, and worlds in the very process of creation! It is amazing to me that I can sit in my home, having had nothing to do with collecting this information (except for paying my taxes), yet have access to these stunning depictions of things I would never be able to see if left to my own devices. The ready availability of information like this is made possible by the understanding we've developed over the last couple of hundred years about a world so small we didn't even know it existed before Joseph Smith's day.

Normally, you and I rely on our five physical senses to gather information about the world around us. And for thousands of years, humans had no way to augment these senses beyond what the unaided sensory organs could perceive. This is why astronomy is the oldest of sciences, because regularities in the heavens could be observed with the naked eye. But with the invention of the telescope, and the microscope around the same time, we began realizing that there existed things in nature that we previously had no idea were there. In the early 1600s, Galileo saw moons circling Jupiter with his primitive telescope; at about the same time, Van Leeuwenhoek saw microorganisms in a droplet of water with his primitive microscope. At first, skeptics claimed that these new observations were not real, that they were a byproduct of some strange aspect of the device itself. But by today, we take it for granted that the things we see through binoculars, telescopes, and microscopes are real—we have faith that our eyes are not being deceived, but that there is a logical explanation for why we can't see these objects without the devices, although we can see them with the devices. Since those early times, our devices have become much more sophisticated, and further and further removed from our natural senses.

Consider the Hubble space telescope photos. I am expected to believe that they represent real objects though the information in those photos has passed through a long series of highly technical steps: light from a distant galaxy is collected with an electronic eye in a space telescope hundreds of miles above the earth; the light is then converted to an electromagnetic signal and beamed to earth; this signal is then converted by computer to a picture on a web page; the picture is then transmitted over a glass fiber to my computer and displayed on an LED screen; that screen then emits light that reaches my natural eye. I could never have seen this galaxy with my own eye. Instead, I must rely on an extremely complex sequence of technical devices over which I have no personal control (nor personal understanding for the most part) that make it possible to extend the range of my perception enormously. In the end, of course, for me to appreciate this wonder, I still have to fall back on the same source of information as did our ancient ancestors: my natural eye. I see what is on the computer screen, and I have faith that all the intervening steps by which this information was transmitted from Hubble to my eye are reliable and present to me a true representation. I see it, so I believe it, yet I'm also tossing in a good helping of faith in all the steps that went into bringing the image of that galaxy to my eye.

The idea that seeing is believing has been around throughout history and is especially prevalent today. Modern people often express pride in not believing in the unseen, the spirits or gods that our ancestors believed in so strongly. Yet they simultaneously take for granted the existence of all kinds of other things that none of us has personally seen or perceived in any way. The new unseen worlds are made up not of spirits and gods, but of microbes, atoms, and photons. And it takes some real faith to believe in these things.

Throughout history, people have always had a strong feeling that there is more to the world than what we can perceive. From ancient times, this suspicion has strengthened belief in the existence of unseen worlds, of gods, of spirits, of angels, and so on. This sense that there is more to the world than the eye can see is so pervasive and irresistible that it has formed the basis for the virtually universal flourishing of religious belief, both in place and time, throughout history. Indeed, C. S. Lewis identifies this universal human need to believe in the unseen as one of the strongest proofs of the existence of God.[1] Yet not everyone believes in God, and often science is held up as a counterpoint to such a belief. To help us understand, let's put our own day into some historical context.

As we saw in the previous chapters, in the century leading up to Joseph Smith's time, Newton's discovery of universal mechanics seemed to cast doubt on the need for the traditional Christian God to explain the world. Among philosophers, this crisis of faith, coupled with other social and religious tensions, brought in the so-called Age of Enlightenment. The new idea was that people can and should rely on their own senses and their own reason to understand the world, leaving aside out-of-date beliefs in the supernatural. In the realm of natural science, this meant relying solely on the maxim "Seeing is believing." Of course, the seeing included augmented seeing, such as observing through telescopes or microscopes. In the end, if the information entered the brain through one of the five sensory organs, that information, and only that information, was to be taken as reliable.

This maxim was sorely tested, however, with the revival around Joseph Smith's time of the concept of the atom. Anciently some Greek natural philosophers like Democritus had proposed the idea that objects were composed of tiny indivisible particles called *atoms* (derived from the Greek word for *uncuttable*). But as we saw in an earlier chapter, these pre-Socratic scientists had been pushed aside by a later, more Zeus-friendly lot including Aristotle. It wasn't until the early nineteenth century that the atomic model was seriously revived.[2]

It was clear from the beginning that atoms had to be extremely small—so small, in fact, that they could not be seen by the best light microscope. After all, objects like glass composed of atoms have very smooth surfaces, which do not feel grainy. Maybe you didn't realize that we still can't see atoms through the best light microscopes, and current theory suggests that it is impossible to ever "see" them through any microscope using visible light. Yet, beginning in Joseph Smith's day, indirect evidence accumulated showing that atoms must exist; and throughout the nineteenth century the whole science of chemistry gradually grew up based on the proposed but unproven existence of atoms. Chemists couldn't see atoms, but experience taught them that they were there. Indeed, when the so-called proof that atoms exist finally arrived (thanks to Einstein), even that was indirect proof based on his explanation of Brownian motion.

Ever heard of Brownian motion? Maybe not. It's an interesting phenomenon. If you suspend tiny solid particles like pollen grains in water and look at them under a powerful light microscope, they seem to dance around as if they were alive. This phenomenon had been observed since Joseph Smith's day and had been dubbed Brownian motion. But it wasn't until the early twentieth century that Einstein was able to quantitatively describe how this motion happened. His model showed that tiny invisible water molecules must be dancing and jiggling very fast and bumping into the visible pollen grains in random fashion (like tiny bumper cars), making the pollen appear to dance around. This was one of Einstein's earliest major contributions to science. It was considered the definitive proof that atoms and molecules exist; but notice that it does not involve actually seeing the atoms, but only their effect.

It wasn't until the end of the twentieth century that scientists were able to come up with the first images of atoms. Notice that I use the word *image* rather than *photograph*, because light wasn't used at all. Instead, a device called a scanning tunneling microscope was used. Calling it a microscope is somewhat misleading, however. It does not have a lens, and a person doesn't look through it. Instead, it is a machine that works something like an old phonograph. A tiny stylus is drawn back and forth across a solid surface, and the atoms of the surface cause variations in an electric current as the stylus moves up and down over the bumpy atoms. These resulting movements are recorded electronically, and a map of the surface is created, each bump representing an atom.

The point is that even to this day, no one has ever seen an atom with his or her eye. That's because atoms have a diameter of about 0.000000004 inches, whereas the human eye sees with a resolution of about 0.004 inches, and the limit of a light microscope is about 0.000008 inches. It takes about 300,000,000,000,000,000,000 atoms to make up a tiny grain of sand. That's nearly as many stars as in the known universe—a bit ironic, since we have used grains of sand to illustrate the vast number of stars!

Atoms are just too small to see. Yet no one, except maybe some members of the flat earth society, doubts the existence of atoms. Why? Because we have all kinds of indirect evidence that atoms exist. And as a result of this belief, and a very elaborate understanding of how these atoms must behave, we have all of the wonders of modern-day life: the metals that make up our cars and our planes; the plastics that make up our clothes and our toys; the fertilizers and other chemicals that help grow our crops; the drugs that protect us from disease; the electronics that keep us from getting bored; the cooling and heating devices that keep us comfortable. All of these are the fruits of our faith in and reliance on the atomic model. Yet not one of us has ever actually seen an atom.

Faith is something we usually attribute to religion, not science. And for this reason, scientists might be more likely to say we have *confidence* in our reliance on the atomic model rather than *faith*, but the difference is really only semantic. Paul said that faith is the "substance of things hoped for, the evidence of things not seen" (Hebrews 11:1). That's exactly what we have for atomic theory— evidence without actually seeing.

The atomic model is only one of many instances in science where we are called upon to believe in things we can't actually see or perceive with one of our natural senses. In our religion, we are also called upon to believe in worlds and phenomena that the eye can't see: our Father in Heaven, Christ, angels, the spirit world. In what ways are the two situations similar and in what ways different?

Scientists would rightly remind us that there is a difference between those ideas for which we have faith in science and those for which we have faith in religion. In science, faith in a particular model or proposition is developed over time through reproducible experimental outcomes. Where possible, these outcomes or experimental results are preferably collected using numerical measurements so that mathematical models can be developed, which show clearly the relationship between cause and effect.

As an example, let's say I propose a scientific hypothesis based on the outcome of an experiment. How are my claims evaluated and ultimately accepted by the scientific community, and ultimately by myself, as valid? There are basically three steps in this process: First, when I report my experiment, other scientists will *peer review* my ideas and make sure they make sense. Second, if other scientists carry out the same experiment in the same way, or in a different way, and get the same result, that lends further support to my claims. Finally, in the end, if my idea shows itself to have predictive and functional value, like atomic theory explaining the mysterious Brownian motion and making possible the existence of my cell phone, that may make my claim Nobel-worthy. (By the way, Einstein didn't get the Nobel prize for explaining Brownian motion, but for another idea entirely.) In these three ways, scientific ideas are evaluated and verified.

In the religious sphere, we also believe in things we cannot see: the existence of God, the spirit world, and the Resurrection, for example. However, we don't have such a formal method for evaluating our claims about such things. Or do we? If you think about it, we use some similar methods to evaluate religious claims as scientific claims, even though we don't normally consider them in these terms. The process isn't the same, but it is not altogether different from that used in science. First, we are exhorted to experiment upon the word of God in scriptures such as Alma 32. Our whole life can be an experiment by following the precepts of the gospel and observing what kind of outcomes it produces for us, both in the short and the long terms. Our faith is developed over time by repeated experiment on the word. Second, we have priesthood and other leaders, including parents who can help us evaluate whether these claims make sense in light of all we know. They can help us compare these outcomes to those obtained by others—this is one of the purposes for which we have a church, a congregation of people all carrying out the same experiment and comparing results. And third, we can see by long-term experience what kinds of predictive and functional value these principles have in shaping not only our own lives but those of our family, friends, and others.

Since we can't see the things of God with our natural eyes, how can we confirm their existence? We are going to have to look for their indirect effects, just as we had to do to firm up our faith in the existence of atoms. The process begins when we are told by someone who has experienced the unseen in some way and we wish to confirm their assertions. This may be a prophet who claims to have experienced the divine firsthand (perhaps as recorded in scripture), or it may be another believer. We begin our own inquiry by carrying out an experiment, as Alma suggests:

> But behold, if ye will awake and arouse your faculties, even to
> an experiment upon my words, and exercise a particle of faith,

yea, even if ye can no more than desire to believe, let this desire work in you, even until ye believe in a manner that ye can give place for a portion of my words. (Alma 32:27)

In this case, we won't be using test tubes or telescopes; instead the experiment is life itself. And what should we do, and what kind of observables should we look for? The scriptures outline the experiment—rely on the word of God and follow in the path of Christ. And they outline what to look for: Paul says the fruits of the spirit are "love, joy, peace, long-suffering, gentleness, goodness, faith, meekness, and temperance" (Galatians 5:22–23).

Now of course in science, we would try to keep things simple by limiting the number of variables so that we can see individual effects and relate them clearly to the cause—we would look at one effect at a time, like the effect of abstaining from alcohol. And we would look at that effect alone for a while in the lives of several people. Beyond that, we would try to measure the outcomes numerically (quantitatively).

But this is real life, and we have to take life as it comes with many effects in the form of life experiences occurring simultaneously—we can't use humans as lab guinea pigs. Furthermore, it isn't realistic to think that we can reduce our level of joy or meekness or spiritual health to numbers. Perhaps you have had the same difficulty as have I in answering questions on health-related questionnaires—the so-called self-reporting method of evaluating a person's state of mind. I may report my happiness quotient as 7 on a scale of 1–10 today, but tomorrow, when I realize I owe a lot of money to the IRS, I might report a 3. It is true that statisticians and psychologists have made progress in devising methods to overcome these problems, but only to some degree, and mostly to large populations rather that to individuals.

In the end, we don't have the luxury of doing the experiment of life in the rigorously scientific way. But the experiment can be done, and the observer (namely you) will have to take the measurements in your own way and evaluate them as best you can. Then you can look to the other two methods of evaluation, peer review by leaders and respected family members, and the long-term practical effects of the conclusions you draw. Many have followed these steps (although most don't think of the process in these terms) and have come to conclude that the evidence most strongly indicates the existence of God and his gospel and the fruits that derive from them.

Of course, the fruits of living by true principles as taught in Christ's gospel are not confined to practicing members of the restored Church of Jesus Christ or even practicing Christians in general. As we will discuss in a subsequent chapter, God operates by immutable laws, and as a loving Father to all mankind, he shares his spirit and the fruits thereof with all who merit its reception through righteous choices. But since his objective is not only "love, joy, peace, long-suffering," and so forth for his children during their mortal lives, but the expansion of these blessings into the eternities, he offers enlargement of these blessings to those who choose to know him and strive to become like him. This choice comes about by means of another experiment, this time upon the veracity of the Book of Mormon as described in Moroni 10:4. The book provides the fulness of Christ's gospel message but also serves as a touchstone for identifying God's designated servant, Joseph Smith, who has the right and power to lead us along the narrow path toward eternal increase. The promise is that if we ask with real intent, the truthfulness of the book will be manifest by a warmth of feeling induced by the Holy Ghost and that this testimony will serve as a firm footing on that path—again, indirect but identifiable evidence of the existence of a world of possibilities we cannot yet see with our eyes. We are not asked for blind faith, but illuminated faith, the same kind of faith scientists have when they talk about electrons.

Perhaps you can see from these examples that both science and religion ask us to trust in indirect evidence, and that some similarities exist between how science and religion both go about verifying the existence of things the eye can't see.

When you think about it, not even nature itself gives us the promise that all factors responsible for natural events will be observable to us. For example, we have already discussed the faith that scientists have in the atomic model, which we accept without question because there is so much circumstantial evidence that atoms exist. We use the atomic model to explain why many things happen in nature without actually *seeing* atoms—nature has hidden them from the human eye, and so it isn't readily obvious that they are a factor in the way materials behave. Now let's consider an even more dramatic example where nature has hidden from our eyes important factors that influence the entire cosmos. They are called dark matter and dark energy.

You may recall that it was just one hundred years ago that Edwin Hubble discovered that ours is not the only galaxy in the cosmos. What I did not remind you about was his other great discovery—that all the galaxies were moving away from one another at very high speed. Since that time, we've learned a lot more about galaxies, some of it very troubling.

First, we've learned recently that there isn't enough mass in the stars, planets, gas, and dust in each galaxy for the resulting gravity to hold the galaxy together, even with the mass of the recently discovered supermassive black hole found at the center of almost every galaxy. Without going into a lot of detail, the best that scientists have been able to come up with to resolve this dilemma is to postulate that there is extra mass in each galaxy that we cannot see with any kind of light, this hidden mass adding enough gravity to hold the galaxy together. In fact, there must be much more hidden mass in each galaxy than matter that we can see. What makes up this hidden mass? We have no idea. We can't see it or detect it with any instrument. Consequently, it has been given the name *dark matter*, not because it is evil, but because we can't see it and don't know what it is.

Second, we have learned just in the last couple of decades that not only are the galaxies moving away from each other, their retreat is accelerating. How can this be? Shouldn't gravity be pulling them together, and thus shouldn't their retreat be slowing down? Again, the best that scientists have been able to come up with is that there is a hidden kind of energy that is like the opposite of gravity pushing the galaxies apart. They call it *dark energy* because we can't observe it directly and we don't know what it is. Nature has hidden this cause from us also.

It turns out that if scientists are interpreting the observations correctly, dark matter and dark energy must make up about 95 percent of all that there is in the universe. What a disappointment! All this time we thought we had made huge progress in understanding the natural world, and it turns out we have been looking at only 5 percent of it all along!

What we are learning from these developments is that just because our senses and our instruments fail to detect things, just because we can't see them, doesn't mean that they don't exist. In fact, science takes it on faith that they do exist because we can see their effects. Perhaps we should be more willing to give the claims of religion the same benefit— more on this later.

In the last chapter, we talked about the majesty of God's creations on the scale of the very large, but as we've introduced here, there's just as much to be said and it is just as amazing to look at it from the other end of the spectrum, on the scale of the very small. Take just one of those grains of sand we talked about earlier. Even this is a true marvel of complexity. As stated, each grain contains about the same number of atoms as there are stars in the known universe. They are arranged in neat rows, linked by electrons that dance in amazing wheels of choreography around a central nucleus. If you were the size of an atom and could look about you within one of these tiny sand grains, you would see rank upon rank of atoms lined up like soldiers on parade extending outward as far as the eye could see in all directions. In fact, at this scale you could journey for years through the matrix and never find an edge. You would be in a little world which seemed to go on forever.

The world of atoms as depicted in those school chemistry texts looks static and lifeless, but the real world of atoms would be in constant motion, the atoms jiggling and colliding and forming and breaking bonds to each other in a frenzied kaleidoscope of constant change. Only now through sophisticated computer graphics are we beginning to be able to depict how this amazing world works. Newly-revealed knowledge of the miniature world presents another witness, a tiny but powerful witness, to the existence of a creator, to the grandeur of God's laws and the care with which he has designed this amazing universe.

And then there is you. You may not be able to see it, but believe it or not, as befits a child of God, your body is the most complex system in the whole universe. The more we learn about the cells that make you up, and the biochemical processes that make you function, the more awe-inspiring you become. Every cell in your body is an amazing little world of its own, with gates and walls, with sophisticated chemical factories, with a central government and a complex communications system. If you could be the size of a protein molecule and set out to explore a single cell in your body, you could spend a lifetime observing all the comings and goings and the busy activity and never run out of interesting new things to see. The experience would make Disneyland look pale by comparison. And you have a hundred trillion such cells of hundreds of different kinds doing lots of different things!

Anyone who has seen a video of circulating blood knows what a complex and awe-inspiring sight it is to see a living system in action at the cellular level. Again, we share this sense of awe about the natural unseen world with non-believers. In the television series *Cosmos*, Sagan says, "We are each of us a multitude. Within us is a little universe."[3] For Latter-day Saints, the complexity of the biological world and the realm of the atom, unseen to our unaided eye, provides another witness of the greatness of our Father in Heaven and his creative genius.

Science has opened up a wondrous view into worlds of existence that we cannot perceive with any of our natural senses. Today, we take the existence of these worlds as a given, in part due to the expansion of our senses through the use of amazing scientific tools, and in part due to the existence of overwhelming indirect evidence. Indeed, we have come to rely on the fruits of our knowledge related to the worlds of atoms, molecules, and biological cells to keep us alive, healthy, and well-stocked with comforts, entertainments, and toys. By the same token, our religion teaches us of the existence of hidden worlds, which those who make the effort to come to know also take as a given. These latter worlds are experienced in direct, dramatic ways by few—the prophets. Their testimonies direct others to experiment and come to experience these worlds by subtle interactions with the spirit and also by indirect evidence, as they yield tangible fruits of love, joy, peace, and fulfilment. By faith science recognizes the worlds of the atom and dark matter, and by faith religion recognizes the worlds of God and the spirit. Neither philosophy is exempt from the need for faith in the existence of the unseen. Indeed, neither could function without it.

NOTES

1. I highly recommend C. S. Lewis's book *Mere Christianity*, first published in 1952 and still in print from HarperOne Publishers.
2. Though it went out of favor, the idea that the world was made up of atoms, sometimes referred to as corpuscles, did not die altogether. It was adhered to by the so-called Epicureans and popped up now and again over the centuries with little serious evidence to give it traction until Joseph Smith's day.
3. Carl Sagan, *Cosmos*, Digitally Remastered Disc Collector's Edition, Cosmos Studios Inc., 2000.

Chapter 5

KINGDOMS AND SPACE

For the Lord giveth wisdom: out of his mouth cometh knowledge and understanding. (Proverbs 2:6)

I think we can all agree that the scriptures are not scientific texts. Yet on occasion, the scriptures make reference to principles that overlap with scientific topics. These points of overlap are often the source of potential apparent conflict between science and religion and can be a stumbling block to those who question their authenticity as divinely inspired. Such a passage occurs in Doctrine and Covenants 88. It is one that you have probably read before, wondered for a passing moment what it meant, and then moved on.

Section 88 of the Doctrine and Covenants is especially rich with scientifically interesting allusions, but let's focus here on this particularly unique one:

> All kingdoms have a law given; and there are many kingdoms; for there is no space in which there is no kingdom; and there is no kingdom in which there is no space, either a greater or a lesser kingdom. And unto every kingdom is given a law; and unto every law there are certain bounds also and conditions . . . Behold, all these are kingdoms, and any man who hath seen any or the least of these hath seen God moving in his majesty and power. (D&C 88:36–38,47)

What do you suppose the Lord is referring to when he speaks of "kingdoms"? And what exactly does he mean when referring to space and kingdoms? In fact, you may have read these verses many times and wondered, like me, what on earth is he talking about? As you will see, this passage only makes sense in light of scientific discoveries made long after Joseph Smith was gone, and as a result, this rather obscure passage has become for me a very strong testimony that Joseph was speaking God's words and not his own.

It strikes me that in Joseph Smith's day, although this passage might have sounded rather grand, it probably didn't make sense to anyone. How could it? In that day, the scientific community, along with everybody else, was quite confident that the universe described by Newton was well understood. The solar system was organized with the sun at the center, the planets circling in elliptical orbits held by universal gravity, and beyond existed a large number of stars, which were other suns, perhaps organized into one spiral galaxy. Between all these heavenly objects was space, which in turn was filled with a massless foggy material called the luminiferous aether. The latter material had never been observed directly but was assumed to exist for two reasons: (1) Nature abhors a vacuum, as Aristotle famously expounded; and (2) There had to exist some kind of material medium for light to travel through as a wave to make its way between objects in space, as discussed in the next chapter.

At the other extreme, that of the very small, little was understood at the time, though as we saw in the previous chapter, the idea of materials being composed of atoms was being nourished in its infancy. Yet, at this tiny scale as well, it was assumed that the atoms filled all the spaces within the object, leaving no voids, which might upset Aristotle. And as mentioned previously, how much of this advanced thinking had made its way into the rough American interior of the 1830s, and more specifically into the purview of Joseph Smith, is hard to say.

But whether Joseph was up to date with the current scientific thought of his day remains irrelevant. The fact is that scientific thinking about space and matter has changed drastically since then, only to reveal that this passage in Doctrine and Covenants is amazingly in line with the science not of Joseph's day, but that of the twenty-first century.

Over the last couple of hundred years, we have learned that the distance between objects in the universe is huge almost beyond comprehension, starting with our own solar system. If the sun were the size of a basketball, the earth would be the size of a marble 170 feet away, and Neptune (the furthest planet) the size of a plump cherry about a mile away. Clearly, most of the solar system is empty space. But that's nothing compared to the distance between stars. The closest star to our sun (Alpha Centauri and its close star neighbors) is about four light years away. A light year is the distance light travels through a vacuum in a year, about 6,000,000,000,000 (that's six trillion) miles. So, on our model with the basketball-size sun, the volleyball representing that star would be 8,600 miles away from our basketball sun (about the distance from Salt Lake City to Melbourne, Australia). With all this in mind, it is estimated that our galaxy is 99.999999999999% empty space! And beyond that, the space between the galaxies dwarfs even this in scope. Indeed, our galaxy is about 100,000 light years across, whereas the distance to the next large galaxy, Andromeda, is about 2.5 million light years! Aristotle loses—there's vacuum everywhere.

What about atoms? The modern model of the structure of the atom dates to the early twentieth century, long after Joseph's day. We've learned that atoms are not solid balls or blocks with no voids in between atoms but instead are spherical balls composed mostly of fluff. The vast majority of the mass of an atom is concentrated in a tiny nucleus at the center (1/100,000th the size of the atom as a whole), which is surrounded by a few extremely tiny electrons that move about so fast we usually refer to them as an electron cloud. That leaves 99.999999999999% of the volume of the atom as empty space. Aristotle loses again!

So, in a nutshell, even the tiny percentage of the universe occupied by matter itself (atoms) is almost completely empty space. It turns out the universe we know is composed mostly of nothing. And that's something no one imagined in Joseph Smith's day. In his day, to claim that there is no kingdom in which there is no space seemed to make no sense. Today, it surely does.

As a scientist, it seems pretty clear to me that Joseph was using the word *kingdom* in a very generic sense to refer to any physical realm of existence, be it in outer space or inner space, be it a galaxy, a planet, or an atom. What then does he mean when he states that there is no space in which there is no kingdom? Are we back to Aristotle again with every void being filled with something?

Joseph taught that there are many things in the universe beyond what we can perceive with our natural senses, as we discussed in the previous chapter. One of these is the so-called spirit of God. We'll discuss this at length in the next chapter, but for now, let's remind ourselves that in another part of the same section of the Doctrine and Covenants, he shares an insight about this particular kingdom. He speaks of this spirit or light as a substance that "proceeds forth from the presence of God to fill the immensity of space." (D&C 88:12) There is certainly plenty of room for it between the atoms and the stars.

What does science now teach us about the space within atoms and within and between galaxies? Lots—much of it speculative at this point. First, you will recall that just in the last few decades, scientists have postulated that a huge amount of *dark matter* and *dark energy* must exist. Presumably, these are spread throughout creation at varying concentrations in various places. Indeed, whatever they are, they are probably all around you this very moment, even though you can't see them or feel them. You see, dark matter and dark energy are invisible to us because they don't interact with normal matter the way normal matter interacts with itself. So, in case you are worried, these things have little or no perceivable effect on your body. They would pass right through you without your even knowing—there's certainly plenty of empty space within your atoms to allow it. Nonetheless, maybe it makes you feel a bit uncomfortable knowing that they are there.

We know so little about dark matter that it undoubtedly will be the fodder for innumerable science fiction novels. Imagine, for example, that dark matter can be organized into the dark matter counterpart of molecules and even life. There could be a dark matter family or dark matter dinosaurs living in your home and moving around, passing through you and your furniture—you completely unaware of them, and they completely unaware of you, with plenty of room to spare for both your worlds to avoid one another.

Setting aside this glib excursion into the realm of plausible science fiction, perhaps you have noticed that what we have learned about the nature of matter and space solves a long-standing mystery about the so-called spirit world. Joseph Smith taught that the spirit world was not in some distant spot in the universe, but right here and around us. For a long time after, this idea was ridiculed as completely incompatible with scientific knowledge. No longer. Not only do we know there's plenty of space for other kingdoms besides our own right here, but now physicists themselves are talking about previously unknown materials residing right amid what is all around us. Please don't misunderstand—I'm not proposing that dark matter is spirit or that the spirit world is made of dark matter. What I am saying is that whereas Joseph's religious claims of a spirit world right here previously made no sense scientifically, now these claims are perfectly compatible with science, and similar claims are being made by scientists themselves.

Believe it nor not, those aren't the most revolutionary ideas about space coming from science nowadays. Here are a few more:

- We once thought space was, by definition, the absence of everything, in other words nothingness—the empty backdrop against which material objects played out their actions. Now, thanks to Einstein and others, we model space as being an actual thing, with characteristics like stretchiness. This aspect of space is essential for explaining the expansion of the universe. Remember that Hubble found that the galaxies are moving away from each other? That's not an exactly correct way to describe what is happening. Instead, we describe the galaxies as embedded in space, and the space itself is expanding, like blowing up a balloon, making it appear that the galaxies are in motion. Really, they are being carried outward as passengers on the expanding space express.

- This idea of expanding space has led to the belief that the universe began 13.7 billion years ago, zooming out from the size of a point in what is called the *big bang*. The reasoning is that if you run the expansion we see today backward in time, at some time in the past everything must have been collapsed down to a point. This idea is still being debated and refined, and maybe the universe was never really as small as a point, but rather just quite a bit smaller than now.

- The expansion of space is coupled with time. The current model, proposed by Einstein, requires that there be four dimensions rather than the three we are accustomed to. We'll talk about time and the mysterious fourth dimension in a subsequent chapter.

- One of the most bizarre proposals about space is that it is imbued with a kind of hidden energy that can spontaneously generate physical particles out of *thin space*.

- And even more bizarre is speculation by serious scientists that there are many universes; and further, that there may be a different universe inside every electron or black hole in our universe.

Some of these ideas circulating today among scientists may strike you as bizarre and contrary to common sense. To quote Einstein, who was the pioneering champion of challenging common sense, "Common sense is the collection of prejudices acquired by age eighteen." [1] In other words, since the early twentieth century, science is now prepared to accept what seem to be nonsensical ideas as long as they have some logical underpinnings. And what is good for the goose ought to be good for the gander. In other words, religion should be offered the same generous berth for its claims, which might seem nonsensical to some. In Joseph Smith's day, it was easy for secular intellectuals to ridicule religious belief in unseen worlds as superstitious nonsense, but it would be, and is, hypocritical for them to do so today.

Let's now consider that portion of the Doctrine and Covenants 88 quote that reads, "And unto every kingdom is given a law; and unto every law there are certain bounds also and conditions . . ." Once again, this passage holds much deeper significance in light of what we know today about the world than was true in Joseph Smith's day. The implication here is that different laws apply to different realms of existence. Perhaps Joseph's contemporaries thought this passage referred to different planets or nations, or to different effects of law on heavenly bodies versus objects on the earth. Like most scriptures, this passage can have multiple levels of meaning. But it certainly carries deep meaning for scientists in the twenty-first century.

Scientists parse the different forces that are responsible for all the phenomena in nature into four categories:

- gravity, with which we all grapple on a familiar basis every time we get out of bed
- electromagnetism, which holds our molecules together and gives us light, heat, and electric bills
- and two nuclear forces, about which we mercifully won't go into in any detail here.

Over the years, scientists researching these various areas have come up with different mathematical models to describe these forces. Some scientists research large objects like stars and galaxies, where gravity plays a big role; others work with extremely small objects like atoms and electrons, where the other three forces dominate. A major problem has arisen when these two fields of research intersect. The models that work for large objects don't dovetail with the models that work for small ones. Ideally, if these models are correct representations of reality, they ought to be compatible, but they aren't. It's as if two teams are working to build a tunnel, each starting from opposite ends, and despite their best planning and intentions, when they get close to one another at the midpoint, the two tunnels don't line up. This is one of the most vexing problems in science right now. It occupied the latter years of Einstein's life, and he couldn't find the answer. Whoever does will be famous.

It would appear that there are different sets of rules that govern the behavior of large objects and small objects in the universe. In the end, it may be that all rules apply to all objects but that some rules influence small objects to a greater extent, and vice versa. But do you notice how this principle is aptly expressed in Doctrine and Covenants 88? "And unto every kingdom is given a law; and unto every law there are certain bounds also and conditions . . ." And beyond the small object / large object difference in scientific law, what about dark matter and dark energy? Clearly, they also have their own sets of rules, which we haven't yet come to understand even at the most superficial level.

This insight, expressed in scripture at a time when none of this science was understood or even imagined, stands as another witness of the inspired nature of Joseph Smith, the backwoods, uneducated prophet.

You may be tempted to think that maybe scientists have got it all wrong. Maybe we have—we should keep an open mind about that. But the Lord promised that in the latter days "God shall give unto you knowledge by his Holy Spirit, yea, by the unspeakable gift of the Holy Ghost, that has not been revealed since the world was until now" (D&C 121:26). And according to Brigham Young, science is one vehicle by which God may reveal truths to his children:

> Every discovery in science and art, that is really true and useful to mankind, has been given by direct revelation from God, though but few acknowledge it. It has been given with a view to prepare the way for the ultimate triumph of truth, and the redemption of the earth from the power of sin and Satan. We should take advantage of all these great discoveries, the accumulated wisdom of ages, and give to our children the

benefit of every branch of useful knowledge, to prepare them to step forward and efficiently do their part in the great work.[2]

The closer we look at nature, the more mind-blowing it appears in our eyes. Maybe that will never end. It is indeed true that "any man who hath seen any or the least of these hath seen God moving in his majesty and power." We have been blessed by fresh insights into the nature of the world in these latter days through both science and prophetic scripture, and it is marvelous to see them coming together in this way.

NOTES

1. Attributed to Albert Einstein in Eric Temple Bell's book, *Mathematics, Queen and Servant of the Sciences*, The Mathematical Association of America, 1952.
2. *Journal of Discourses*, Albert Carrington Pub., 1862, **9**, p. 369; Brigham Young discourse, August 31, 1862.

Chapter 6

LIGHT IN SCIENCE AND THEOLOGY

And if your eye be single to my glory, your whole bodies shall be filled with light, and there shall be no darkness in you; and that body which is filled with light comprehendeth all things. (D&C 88:67)

We humans are drawn to the light. We love to feel the light of the sun on our faces and to admire a beautiful sunset. As we sit around a campfire, we are often mesmerized by the light of the burning embers. And if a light is turned on in a dark room, we turn our heads to witness the source.

There is an amazing correspondence between what modern revelation teaches about light and what science has learned about light since Joseph Smith's day. Let's look carefully at these two sources of knowledge. First, let's review what modern prophets and scriptures teach us.

The word *light* appears 456 times in the standard works, 195 of these in latter-day scripture including the Book of Mormon, the Doctrine and Covenants, and the Pearl of Great Price. Clearly, light plays an important role in the Lord's teachings about the gospel and his creations. And it turns out that modern scripture and revelation clarify the nature of light significantly over what we can learn from the Bible. One particularly salient verse in the Doctrine and Covenants reads:

> For the word of the Lord is truth, and whatsoever is truth is light, and whatsoever is light is Spirit, even the Spirit of Jesus Christ. (D&C 84:45)

This verse is straightforward and profoundly enlightening in its teachings about light and Spirit. Notice that the word of the Lord, truth, light, and Spirit are closely interconnected. We will come back to the "word of the Lord" and "truth" later, but for now, let's focus on the teaching that whatever is light is Spirit, which is the Spirit of Christ. This is an important new insight we gain from modern revelation: not only are light and Spirit connected, but, in fact, light is a type or aspect of Spirit. (We assume that the reason the word *spirit* is capitalized here is out of respect for the Master of that Spirit, our Lord Jesus Christ. It is not usually capitalized in the scriptures.) Notice that not all spirit is equated to light but that all light is spirit, leaving open the possibility that there is more to spirit than the light we see with our eyes alone. In other words, not all spirit is light, but all light is a form of spirit. So that when the scriptures speak of light, we ought to think in our minds that this is a type of spirit. And very often in scripture we see the words *light* and *spirit* used interchangeably.

What is this spirit spoken of? We know that we (including Jesus) lived in the *spirit world* before coming to mortality, and each of us had a *spirit body*. Is the "Spirit of Jesus Christ" spoken of in Doctrine and Covenants 88 Christ's spirit body? Clearly not. Then what is it speaking of? To answer this question, let's turn to another passage from the Doctrine and Covenants:

> There is no such thing as immaterial matter. All spirit is matter, but it is more fine or pure, and can only be discerned by purer eyes; We cannot see it; but when our bodies are purified we shall see that it is all matter. (D&C 131:7–8)

This insight was provided by Joseph Smith not long before his death and is critical to understanding the nature of spirit, and therefore of light. This passage defines spirit, and light as one aspect of spirit, to be a material substance. Calling it "fine" implies that it is made up of very fine particles. The fact that it is seen with "purer eyes" fits well with the concept that spirit is like light in its character, hence the close relationship between the two.

A question that often arises in attempting to understand the nature of this spirit substance has to do with its relation to the Holy Ghost as a person. Sometimes in scripture, the author refers to the Spirit of God, or simply spirit, other times to the Holy Ghost. Are they the same? Are they different? To address this question, we can turn to the writings of apostle James Talmage, who was not only one of the Quorum of the Twelve Apostles, but also a respected scientist. In Talmage's book, *The Articles of Faith*, a work which was commissioned by the First Presidency, he includes a chapter on the Holy Ghost. As part of the discussion, he addresses the question *Is there a difference in scripture between what is referred to as the Holy Ghost versus the Holy Spirit?*

> The term Holy Ghost and its common synonyms, Spirit of God, Spirit of the Lord, or simply, Spirit, Comforter, and Spirit of Truth, occur in the scriptures with plainly different meanings, referring in some cases to the person of God, the Holy Ghost, and in other instances to the power or authority of this great Personage . . .
>
> Much of the confusion existing in human conceptions concerning the nature of the Holy Ghost arises from the common failure to segregate His person and powers. Plainly, such expressions as being filled with the Holy Ghost, and His falling upon persons, have reference to the powers and influences that emanate from God, and which are characteristic of Him; for the Holy Ghost may in this way operate simultaneously upon many persons even though they be widely separated, whereas the actual person of the Holy Ghost cannot be in more than one place at a time. Yet we read that through the power of the Spirit, the Father and the Son operate in their creative acts and in their general dealings with the human family. The Holy Ghost may be regarded as the minister of the Godhead, carrying into effect the decisions of the Supreme Council.[1]

Thus, we find reference in scripture to two entities, the Holy Ghost, who is a personage of spirit, and the spirit substance, of which spirit bodies and the spirit world are composed. This spirit, and the light associated with it, as referenced in scripture, is a very powerful force in nature, as described in another passage in Doctrine and Covenants 88. Speaking of Christ, we read:

> He that ascended up on high, as also he descended below all things, in that he comprehended all things, that he might be in all and through all things, the light of truth; Which truth shineth. This is the light of Christ. As also he is in the sun,

and the light of the sun, and the power thereof by which it was made. As also he is in the moon, and is the light of the moon, and the power thereof by which it was made; As also the light of the stars, and the power thereof by which they were made; And the earth also, and the power thereof, even the earth upon which you stand. And the light which shineth, which giveth you light, is through him who enlighteneth your eyes, which is the same light that quickeneth your understandings; Which light proceedeth forth from the presence of God to fill the immensity of space—The light which is in all things, which giveth life to all things, which is the law by which all things are governed, even the power of God who sitteth upon his throne, who is in the bosom of eternity, who is in the midst of all things. (D&C 88:6–13)

So, in summary, modern revelation teaches us that light is a kind of spirit matter, that the two terms are often used interchangeably, that it is material composed of fine particles, that it fills the immensity of space, that it is in all things and gives them law and life, and that it constitutes the very power of God, emanating forth from him to all his creations. There is much more to be learned about light and spirit, and for your edification, I would refer you to the fifth chapter of Parley P. Pratt's *Key to the Science of Theology,* published twenty years after Joseph's death by one of his closest confidants. Here's a short excerpt:

This leads to the investigation of that substance called the Holy Spirit.

As the mind passes the boundaries of the visible world, and enters upon the confines of the more refined and subtle elements, it finds itself associated with certain substances in themselves invisible to our gross organs, but clearly manifested to our intellect by their tangible operations and effects. . . .

The purest, most refined and subtle of all these substances, and the one least understood, or even recognized, by the less informed among mankind, is that substance called the Holy Spirit.

This substance, like all others, is one of the elements of material or physical existence, and therefore subject to the necessary laws which govern all matter as before enumerated.

Like all other elements, its whole is composed of individual particles. Like them, each particle occupies space, possesses the power of motion, requires time to move from one part of space to another, and can in no wise occupy two spaces at once. In all these respects it differs nothing from all other matter.

This substance is widely diffused among the elements of space. This Holy Spirit, under the control of the Great Eloheim, is the grand moving cause of all intelligences, and by which they act.[2]

Now for comparison let's examine the evolution of our understanding of the nature of light through science. I say evolution, because in fact scientific ideas about light have taken a few turns over the years. Until the twentieth century, there was an ongoing debate over whether light was a particle or a wave. There was conflicting evidence for both models. In the eighteenth century, Newton thought of light as particulate; his contemporary Huygens, in Holland, described it as a wave. By Joseph Smith's day, one hundred years or so later, the wave model was considered the winner, and there was widespread agreement, though not unanimity, in the scientific community, that this model was well established. Of course, the question arose: what is waving? This is an especially acute problem when you consider light traveling through empty space. You can't have a wave in nothing, just as you couldn't have a water wave in an empty bathtub. But this problem was neatly addressed by theorizing that space must be filled with an undetectable material called the *luminiferous aether*. The prevailing scientific thinking about light in Joseph's day was that it was an *electromagnetic wave*. (More on *electromagnetic* later.)

Once again, we find that Joseph Smith's bold claims in his revelations that light is a particulate substance flew in the face of the accepted scientific thought of his day. He had a habit of doing this, as you may have noticed.

Yet, as the twentieth century rolled around, science decided to change its mind. A new set of theories arose to describe the unseen miniature world of the atom and its interactions with light, a theory called *quantum mechanics*. This subject is highly mathematical and strikes terror in the hearts of most college students, but its basic principle is quite straightforward. It is the idea that some things in nature can be broken down only so far, that nature is fundamentally grainy at its smallest dimensions. We have all encountered this principle in everyday life, as we find that some things we encounter are *quantized*. For example, you may carry some coins in your pocket; you may have 3 pennies or 5 pennies, but you would never offer 2½ pennies to someone. Pennies are quantized in this way. By the same token, your eyes are quantized—you probably have exactly two, not a little bit more or less. And similarly, atoms are quantized. You can have 1 atom of copper or 10 atoms, but not 5.7 atoms.

The new theory of light in the twentieth century was that light is also quantized—that it is particulate in nature. These particles were given a name: *photons*, from which is derived the fictional weapon, *photon torpedo*, familiar to all Star Trek fans. A photon is an indivisible packet of light energy, and different kinds of light, like red light or blue light, have photons that contain different discreet amounts of energy. Each photon of red light has less energy than each photon of blue light. And the word *light* includes not just the kind of photons we see with our eyes, but also infrared, ultraviolet, radio, x-ray, and other kinds of light.

This particulate model of light is now deeply rooted in scientific thought and squares nicely with the description of light we find in latter-day revelation as described above by Joseph Smith. In Joseph's day, there appeared to be a conflict between his revelations and science; by the twenty-first century, that apparent conflict has been resolved in favor of revelation. Both agree that light is particulate in nature.

As mentioned above, Joseph's revelations also imply that there is more to light than meets the eye, to use a common phrase. In Joseph's day, when people, including scientists, used the word *light* they were referring to the light we can see with our natural eyes. Although infrared and ultraviolet light were just being discovered, it was not at all clear then, as it is now, that visible light is only a small part of the broad spectrum of kinds of light that exist, differentiated by how much energy is contained in an individual photon of each kind. Just to illustrate, if we chart the different kinds of light, ranging from radio waves at the lower energy end, to gamma rays at the upper energy end, the kind of light visible to our eyes would just be a tiny band close to the middle of the chart. Most kinds of light are invisible to us.

Infrared light, which has an energy just smaller than visible light and which we don't perceive with our eyes as light, but with our nerves as heat, was discovered just before Joseph's day in Europe. Traditional incandescent light bulbs give off ninety percent of their energy not in the form of visible light, but in the form of infrared light, which we perceive as heat. But did you know that *you* radiate light, that you glow like a light bulb? It's true—your body is a source of light just like a light bulb. But you glow entirely in infrared light, not visible light. That's why an infrared sensitive camera can take your picture in the dark. It turns out that everything in the universe radiates light of some energy, even things that are very cold. If you had eyes that were sensitive to infrared light, you could see other people in the dark. Any being that had eyes that were sensitive to all the different kinds of light would be able to see all physical objects in the universe; nothing made of normal matter (as opposed to dark matter) would be invisible to such a being.

Ultraviolet light, with photon energies just a bit higher than those of visible light, was discovered about the same time as infrared. This is the kind of light that gives us a sunburn, so we try to avoid it by putting on sunscreen. All the other kinds of light, including microwaves, radio waves, x-rays, and gamma rays, were discovered long after Joseph Smith's day. These latter kinds dominate our chart of the electromagnetic spectrum and include the vast majority of energies. So if all light is spirit, we can conclude that there is a lot more to spirit than the light we can see with our eyes, as Joseph's revelations imply, and this principle (even when expressed in scientific terms) was definitely not understood by science in Joseph's day.

There is an even more fundamental aspect of the modern scientific model of light that conforms to a statement in Joseph Smith's revelations but which was not understood in his day. This insight found in latter-day scripture goes right to the heart of one of the most basic principles of science: *electromagnetism*. You may recall that in the previous chapter, we discussed how scientists describe all phenomena in nature based on four fundamental forces, one of which is the so-called electromagnetic force. In Joseph Smith's day, relatively little was understood about either electricity or magnetism. It hadn't been that long since Benjamin Franklin's famous and dangerous investigations of electricity with lightning, kites and keys, and so on. In Italy, Volta had recently reported his experimentation with the simple battery, and Galvani had reported that electricity could make disembodied frog legs jump. On the other hand, magnetism was still considered a mysterious force that could waft through empty space to apply forces on disconnected objects. It wasn't until decades after Joseph's death that James Maxwell in England announced his highly acclaimed theory connecting electricity and magnetism into one model, which described light as an *electromagnetic* phenomenon.

What does this mean? It means that electricity and magnetism are inextricably connected and are manifestations of the same natural process. As time progressed, it became clear that electromagnetism lies at the heart of understanding the inner workings of the atom. In the twentieth century we learned that the atom is made of fundamental particles, with positively charged protons in the nucleus and negatively charged electrons swirling around it. You undoubtedly learned in school that oppositely charged objects attract and that the atom is held together by the attractive force between these oppositely charged particles. The combinations of different atoms in different arrangements that we call molecules are held together by these same forces. All of chemistry, including the biochemistry occurring in your body right now and allowing you to read and understand the words on this page, results from interactions involving this force—the electromagnetic force—in the atoms and molecules of your body. Furthermore, in the twentieth century we came to understand that light, in the form of photons, is the carrier of this force—it is the means by which particles exchange information with each other so that they can interact with each other the way they do, as we will illustrate.

First, though, let me make a confession. In the interest of your sanity, to this point I've shared with you only part of what scientists now hold true about light. Here's the rest of the story. While it is true that in the twentieth century science came to the conclusion that light is particulate, that is not the whole story. Scientists could not simply turn their backs on the fact that sometimes light does things that only waves can do, like refract and diffract (don't worry if these phenomena are not familiar to you—you can always look them up on Wikipedia the next time you have a moment). In an unusual spirit of compromise, science decided to resolve the question of whether light is a particle or a wave by saying it is both—a thing which sometimes behaves as a particle and sometimes as a wave. (If this seeming paradox gives you a headache, you're not alone!) Light is now modeled as an electromagnetic particle-wave or wave-particle, which can travel between other particles like electrons and protons, carrying information between them. Of course, there is a lot more to all this than can be described here, but that is sufficient for us to appreciate the profound nature of what we find almost hidden in a passing comment in Doctrine and Covenants 88. So now that I have cleared my conscience on this matter, let's move on and not worry too much more about it.

We have already quoted the passage in Doctrine and Covenants 88 that alludes to the following principle about light. It is found in verse 11:

> And the light which shineth, which giveth you light, is through him who enlighteneth your eyes, which is the same light that quickeneth your understandings. (D&C 88:11)

Have you ever really stopped and thought carefully about what this verse is trying to convey? I think most of us, like myself, tend to read the scriptures too quickly, whereas if we pondered them more deeply, we would see that there is sometimes a hidden jewel of meaning we might otherwise miss. That is true here. I probably read this verse many times before it finally struck me that this seemingly obscure, and rather odd, statement made perfect sense from a modern scientific point of view. What is said? It says that the same light which we see with our eyes also works in our brains to allow us to think and to understand. Is that true? Yes, by the principles of modern science, but it didn't make a whole lot of sense in Joseph Smith's lifetime.

How is that true? In layman's terms, here's how you see a flower and realize that it is a flower according to twenty-first century science:

- The atoms and molecules in the flower emit or reflect photons of light (electromagnetic radiation) according to strict electromagnetic rules obeyed by its electrons.
- These photons (electromagnetic messengers) travel the distance from the flower to your eye at very high speed.
- The electrons in the molecules in the retina of your eye absorb the photons according to the same electromagnetic rules that the flower used to emit them.
- The retina cells in the eye then pass the information on to the optic nerve cells using the electromagnetic processes of chemistry (via electrons); in essence, an electromagnetic signal is passed to these nerve cells.
- This electromagnetic signal passes along the nerve cells to the brain cells, which are likewise built to conduct electromagnetic signals by passing charged atoms (called *ions*) back and forth to each other.

- The brain cells process the information using the electromagnetic processes of chemistry based on electrical conductance between neurons—aha, this is a flower!

Whether you have a clear or somewhat muddied picture in your mind of this process, I think you can appreciate one thing. All the steps in the process, from the origination of the light in the flower to the final processing in your brain to recognize that it is a flower, involve the same natural principle—electromagnetism. The chemistry of emitting and absorbing light, the transmission of that light through space, and the transmission of electrical signals through nerve and brain cells are all electromagnetic processes working on a common principle. And if you look back at the verse in Doctrine and Covenants 88, you will notice that this concept is perfectly consistent with what is taught there—the light we see with our eyes is the same as that which enlivens our brains and allows us to think. Let me emphasize again that the Doctrine and Covenants is not designed to be a science text, but rather, we can see that what the Lord reveals does not in any way contradict what we know today about nature. Joseph Smith didn't know these things at the time; no one did, because the principles of electromagnetism that govern the behavior of photons and electrons, atoms, and ions, hadn't yet been discovered. But Joseph Smith got it right. To me, this hidden gem of insight is a strong testimony of the inspired nature of modern revelation.

Light is indeed a key to understanding in both theology and science. The vast majority of lessons we have learned about the natural world in science result from our observing the world through light—not only visible light, but all the different kinds of light we've discussed. In fact, we've come to understand that the world we live in is made up largely of two things: atoms and light. And scientists have been extremely creative in inventing devices to allow us to extend our natural senses and observe nature in all the kinds of light our eyes can't see. Historically, science got its start with people looking at the light from the stars. And we are still looking out into the heavens, now with elaborate machines like space telescopes that make it possible for us to see objects far away as they were in the distant past, using all the different kinds of light from gamma-rays to radio waves. Likewise, we have microscopes that use different kinds of light and allow us to probe into the tiny worlds that underpin our everyday world with unimaginable complexity.

Frequent references to light in scripture make it clear that light is one of God's principal gifts to his children to help them live in and navigate this physical world. Ultimately, he and we are creatures of light. He is master of all light and spirit, and Doctrine and Covenants 88 teaches us that it is through this medium that he is able to reach out and govern all his creations. And as his children, we are given this beautiful promise:

> That which is of God is light; and he that receiveth light, and continueth in God, receiveth more light; and that light groweth brighter and brighter until the perfect day. (D&C 50:24)

NOTES

1. James E. Talmage, *The Articles of Faith*, 12th ed., The Church of Jesus Christ of Latter-day Saints, 1969, pp. 159–160.
2. Parley P. Pratt, *Key to the Science of Theology*, 1891 ed., George Q. Cannon and sons Pub., reprinted by Kessinger Publishing, pp. 38–39.

Chapter 7

GOD OF NATURE

It is the first principle of the Gospel to know for a certainty the Character of God. (Teachings of the Prophet Joseph Smith, *p. 345*)

Have you ever been to a magic show? If so, when the magician sawed someone in half or made an elephant disappear before your very eyes, were you amazed? Did you for a moment wonder if maybe the magic was real, or did your common sense tell you that this was just an illusion—that behind the seemingly impossible was an explanation that the magician knew but that was kept hidden from you? Actually, you are probably like most of us—you experienced a thrill at the possibility of the impossible, while at the same time in the back of your mind (or rather in the front of your brain in the frontal lobes of logic) you knew that you were really still in the world of regularity and reason.

In the last few centuries, mankind has gradually been converted to the idea that the world operates on a set of rules that applies to all things at all times. We've come to think this way about everything around us almost without question (except momentarily when we see a magic show perhaps). And therefore, it is hard for us to appreciate that this has not always been the case. It is hard for us today to understand that for most of history, people have not gone about their lives believing that nature here on earth is predictable because it operates on a set of fundamental rules that apply to everything. Instead, for almost all of history, when people looked at the world around them, they envisioned that every event was uniquely driven. Every event had its own individual cause that was dependent not on a set of natural, immutable laws, but rather on the whim of some invisible sentient being—a god or a spirit. When the wind blew, it was not because there was gradation in atmospheric pressures that caused a gas to flow from a region of high pressure to low, but rather because a god or spirit decided to make it blow. If a disease struck, it was not because a microorganism infected the victim, but because a god or spirit chose to inflict the disease. If a harvest was good, it was not because good soil and healthy seed were coupled with regular sunshine and rain, but because a god or a spirit chose to make it so.

This way of thinking in the ancient world (right up until about five hundred years ago in Europe and even later in other parts of the world) was very different from our own. It meant that to the ancients, for all practical purposes, everything was magic. Today we talk about the *supernatural* in an attempt to distinguish what is supposed to happen normally (a natural event) versus what might happen when the laws of nature are circumvented (a *super*natural event). But to the ancients this kind of thinking made no sense. Since every event was independently caused by a supernatural being (which to them simply meant a being who was present but unseen), any event was just as *natural* as any other. For them, the magic show would have been just as fun to watch as for us, but the difference is that they could just as easily believe that the elephant really did disappear as that the wind blew. Admittedly, an elephant disappearing would have seemed unusual to them, but the difference is that they would chalk it up to the god of elephants choosing on a whim that day to do something unusual, perhaps for fun, or perhaps for some other inscrutable reason. Admittedly, they might have been skeptical, but they did not have to completely *suspend disbelief* as we do; instead, they would have found it easy to believe if it came to that.

Of course, even in the ancient world, it seemed that there were special parts of nature that were different in this respect, and those were the heavens. Unlike events here on earth, the heavens did seem to follow regular, predictable patterns that never changed. That is one reason why the heavens were commonly revered, and a reason why the ancient Greeks created a model wherein the heavens operated on completely different principles than things here on the earth. The heavens were predictable and regular; things on earth were unpredictable and operated on whimsy.

You will recall Aristotle's model of the world discussed in an earlier chapter. His view, which dominated western thought for nearly two thousand years, depicted the heavens (everything from the moon outward) as operating by a set of rules that were perfect and unchanging. The planets (including the sun and moon) were embedded in crystalline spheres and rotated in perfect circles around the earth, as did the sphere of the stars. These bodies were composed of a glorious, weightless, immutable substance called the quintessence (the fifth element) and were the dwellings of the eternal gods. The inner workings of this alien realm were not amenable to investigation nor to understanding by lowly human minds. In the Christian middle ages, these gods were replaced by angels and the one God, but the model was left largely unchanged and was adopted as sacred truth by the dominant Christian church. While the spherical heavens were regular and unchanging, the earth, at the center of the universe, was the dumping ground where all heavy materials that were changeable, corrupt, and prone to decay had fallen. Human beings were part of this corrupt earthly place and were therefore mortal and prone to sin. Under the earth, at the very bottom of the universe, was hell.

Unlike events in the unchanging heavens, events on earth did not operate based on regular, unchanging rules. So while you could count on the sun in the heavens rising and setting on a regular basis and the planets wandering through the stars in a predictable way from month to month, you couldn't count on the weather on earth from one day to the next. And this is why it was so important to ancient civilizations like the Egyptians that their king—Pharaoh—be connected to, or perhaps the son of, some heavenly being, like the sun, because it brought some of the regularity found in the heavens down into the chaos of the earth. This way, the Pharaoh might have the power to impose some regularity and predictability normally found only in the heavens onto the pattern of floods of the Nile, for example. And we see this kind of thinking sprinkled through virtually all ancient cultures.

In a nutshell, the ancients thought of the world as divided into two completely different regions: the earth, which was chaotic, and the heavens, which were predictable but incomprehensible to the human mind. Among others, the men largely responsible for changing this world view were Galileo and Newton, as discussed earlier. They showed via evidence and theory that the same set of natural laws that governed the motions of bodies in the heavens also governed the motions of bodies on earth. Newton drove this home with his law of universal gravitation, but since his day, many new principles have been discovered that underpin the actions of all things in the universe, large and small.

I don't think most of us appreciate just how huge a paradigm shift this represents. Think about how you see the world and your life on a day-to-day basis. You wake up in the morning and see the weather forecast on TV. You expect that the meteorologist telling you that it will probably start raining this afternoon might be right. That's because scientific knowledge of the atomic construction of the world, and the way gases in the atmosphere behave, and the way heat energy works in the atmosphere, and the effect of the sun's heat on the atmosphere, and the nature of the light from the sun, and the rotation of the earth, and all the science and math-based engineering that went into sending satellites into space, and our understanding of microwaves and radio waves, which make it possible to communicate information at the speed of light—all these things have come together so neatly that we have enough understanding of the weather that we can make good (although not perfect) predictions. I bet you can think of a thousand ways that you routinely count on the predictability of events in your life due to the fruits of modern science. And we all just take that view of things for granted. We no longer feel at the mercy of total whimsy in nature here on earth. Although we all face some uncertainty in our lives, imagine how different, and how much harder, your life would be if you felt that there was no predictability in the world at all.

You can't blame the ancients for not seeing that nature here on earth is underpinned by regular, predictable rules or laws. Until we had inventions like the telescope and microscope to extend our natural senses, it really wasn't possible to see those patterns. Since the world to them seemed chaotic, and since they could only ascribe the causes of events to the whim of spirits and gods, it is no wonder they devoted themselves to imploring the help of those gods.

What then does all this have to do with the relationship between latter-day revelation and science? It has to do with our understanding of the nature of God and his relationship to the laws of nature. When the ancient Christian church strayed from the pure teachings of Christ's gospel, the traditional view of the world described above led to a completely distorted view of God in this respect. Remember that almost all Christian churches of our day adhere to a doctrine that was developed in the fourth century AD at a council of bishops from around the Roman world. This council was called together by the then pagan Roman emperor Constantine at a town called Nicaea in what is now Turkey. The reason for the council was to come up with a common Christian doctrine, especially about the nature of God. Different Christian communities were warring over the true nature of God, struggling with these kinds of questions:

- If there is only one God, how is it possible for Christ and his Father both to be God?
- How can Christ be a god and at the same time be a mortal man? After all, God is supposed to be perfect.
- What is the Holy Spirit? Is he a person, and if so, how can he also be God?
- What is the relationship between God the Father and Christ?
- In what way is God perfect? Is he part of nature or above nature?

At the command of the Roman emperor, the bishops at Nicaea were not let off the hook until they could agree. And so they did, at least most of them. What they came up with was a document called the Nicene Creed. This creed was modified slightly later, but it has had a strong hold on Christianity ever since.

One of the challenges these bishops had in creating the creed was to make it fit not only with accepted scripture (even the question of what was reliable scripture and what was not was an issue), and with differing opinions of the bishops, but also to make it compatible with the best philosophical thinking of the day. This was an almost impossible task. And the resulting document is not unlike others generated through compromise by committee.

Where questions about philosophy were concerned, the teachings of Plato and Aristotle from the fourth century BC predominated in the fourth century AD. Much has been written about the opinions of these philosophers about the gods, not all of it clear. But the idea that the heavens were the abode of God or gods and that these differed in all respects from earthly things is made evident in the creed produced at Nicaea. God is presented as a being entirely unlike anything earthly, including man, or at least the earthly corporeal aspect of man.

The Council of Nicaea did not end the debate, however. More councils were held, and over later centuries as more denominations of Christianity developed, so did more creeds. One thing most of these creeds share in common is this idea that things in heaven, including God, are utterly unlike anything earthly. For example, it is claimed that it would be inconsistent with the idea that God is perfect for him to have a material body, because physical matter is by its nature corrupt according to the ancient model of the world. And to resolve the question of the relationship between the Father, the Son, and the Holy Ghost, and how they relate to the principle of monotheism, the concept of the trinity was developed in the late fourth century AD. This is essentially the idea that there is one God, but he is manifest in more than one way, in fact in the three ways associated with his three names. This God was by nature entirely *other* and shared none of the characteristics we would consider human; and he was so far above us as to be entirely incomprehensible to the human mind.

For as long as it lasted, the Aristotelian model of the world, with its clear division between heaven and earth, fit well with orthodox Christian doctrine. But when this model began to crumble in the face of new evidence and the development of the Newtonian mechanical model of the world, the long-standing harmony between science and religion began to crumble as well. With time, it became clearer and clearer that the heavens operated on the same set of natural principles as objects on earth, leading to new and unsettling questions. Where now was the abode of God and the angels? Where was hell?

As time went by, and the outer reaches of the universe kept being pushed further outward and back in time by scientific investigation, this gulf between science and religion widened. People were put in the uncomfortable position of having to choose between the two, or to make some kind of accommodation. The most common accommodation was made in religion—to relegate the world of angels, spirits, and God to some other dimension or state of being undetectable to us. You see, in the ancient world, when people referred to God being in his heaven, they knew exactly where that was—it was *up there*, among the stars. You could see it. But now, heaven came to mean something entirely different: an invisible realm you couldn't point to, existing who knows where. And, of course, this tended to distance people even further from a God they already had trouble identifying with, given the doctrine that he was entirely other and incomprehensible to humankind. It became harder to draw close to a God who was so distant he didn't even seem to live in our universe.

Two particular principles found in this traditional Christian theology are important for our discussion here concerning latter-day theology and science:

- God is found outside of nature; he exists above it and independent of it. He created natural law but can contravene it at any point he wishes.
- God is utterly unknowable; he is beyond the capability of the human mind to understand.

This is the state of things as they had developed by Joseph Smith's day in almost every denomination of Christendom. I've told you this story because it helps us to realize just how revolutionary Joseph's revelations were concerning the nature of God—and how much more compatible they were and are with modern science than the traditional view.

Members of The Church of Jesus Christ of Latter-day Saints are sometimes accused of *not being Christians*. This comes as a shock to practicing members because not only is Christ's name in the name of our Church, but it's impossible to attend one of our meetings without hearing the name repeatedly. Indeed, if you look carefully at the Church's Articles of Faith and compare them with the creeds of most mainstream Christian churches, you will see a great deal of overlap, especially concerning the role of Christ in the scheme of things. We share in common the idea that Christ was the son of God, the only begotten of the Father in the flesh, born of the virgin Mary, who made atonement for our sins, who was crucified and resurrected, thereby making it possible for us to live again, who will come again and judge all people, and on and on. But the one area where we differ markedly from mainstream Christianity involves doctrines related to the nature of God. And it is largely because we don't subscribe to the sections of the traditional creeds that deal with this question that we are accused in this way.

In what ways do we differ from other denominations concerning the nature of God? Joseph Smith's very first encounter with the divine occurred in the Sacred Grove in upstate New York, where he saw the Father and the Son. This one brief encounter taught Joseph a great deal about the divine nature. He learned that the Father and the Son are two separate beings with physical bodies in the form of a man. However, there was nothing normal about them in other ways. Their very persons gave off light so bright it defied description.

Over subsequent years and many more revelatory experiences, Joseph came to understand that the Holy Ghost is also a personage with human form, though his body is composed of spirit substance as we have described in the previous chapter. Furthermore, the physical bodies of the Father and the Son differ from our bodies in that they are immortal, eternal, and glorified—in other words somehow coupled with tremendous energy in the form of light that emanates from them to fill all their creations. We learned in the previous chapter that this glorious light or spirit puts them in contact with and in control of all their creations and gives law and life to all things (Doctrine and Covenants 88). Through his spirit, God administers law to all objects in the universe, as described in that section:

> All kingdoms have a law given; And there are many kingdoms; for there is no space in the which there is no kingdom; and there is no kingdom in which there is no space, either a greater or a lesser kingdom. And unto every kingdom is given a law; and unto every law there are certain bounds also and conditions. . . . He comprehendeth all things, and all things are before him, and all things are round about him; and he is above all things, and in all things, and is through all things, and is round about all things; and all things are by him, and of him, even God, forever and ever. And again, verily I say unto you, he hath given a law unto all things, by which they move in their times and their seasons; And their courses are fixed, even the courses of the heavens and the earth, which comprehend the earth and all the planets. And they give light to each other in their times and in their seasons, in their minutes, in their hours, in their days, in their weeks, in their months, in their years—all these are one year with God, but not with man. The earth rolls upon her wings, and the sun giveth his light by day, and the moon giveth her light by night, and the stars also give their light, as they roll upon their wings in their glory, in the midst of the power of God. Unto what shall I liken these kingdoms, that ye may understand? Behold, all these are kingdoms, and any man who hath seen any or the least of these hath seen God moving in his majesty and power. (D&C 88: 36–38, 41–47)

Beyond this, we learn from the Book of Abraham, taken from ancient Egyptian scrolls, that God lives on a planet in the very universe we inhabit. This idea is reiterated in Doctrine and Covenants 130:4–5: "Is not the reckoning of God's time, angel's time, prophet's time, and man's time, according to the planet on which they reside? I answer, yes." Furthermore, he is literally the Father of our spirits, and we are on a path to becoming like him if we so choose.

This is a very different depiction of the nature of God than we find in traditional Christianity, as you can clearly see. Latter-day Saints have been derided for believing in a so-called *anthropomorphic* God (a god with a humanlike physical body) and for their denial of the doctrine of the Trinity. Books could be written, and much has been written, debating the relative merits of the traditional versus the Latter-day Saint viewpoint and which of these is more consistent with Bible scripture. But it is not my task here to attempt to resolve this issue. Instead, I wish to make a simple point: Joseph's theology concerning the nature of God brings him back into the natural universe and makes him a participant in, rather than apart from, nature.

The argument has been made that religion is only an instrument created by humans to fill in the gaps of their understanding of the world. This so-called *God in the gaps* approach implies that God is only a useful temporary tool. By this approach, as science reveals more about the true workings of nature, there is less and less need for a God to explain the parts of nature we don't yet understand. As the gaps diminish, so does the need for God. This mode of thought is a serious threat to traditional Christianity. By contrast, with its belief in a God who lives in and rules nature itself, the theology of the restored Church recognizes no such gaps, and the relevance of God never tarnishes as we learn more about the world. The Father we worship is not above nature, but one with nature, and every natural law he reveals to us through science is simply another step in understanding him and his ways.

So what does this imply about Latter-day Saint understanding of events we would call supernatural? In traditional Christian theology, the God who exists above nature may be seen to intervene into the natural course of things and sidestep natural law at any time. This gives God the same kind of arbitrary power over nature as believed for other gods and spirits anciently. If this thinking is valid, the scientific description that nature follows regular laws is only an illusion; these laws can be countermanded at any time in any way for any reason deemed appropri- ate by God. When this happens, we would say that a supernatural event has occurred, a miracle, because it is *super*-natural, the root meaning being *above nature*.

Can you see how this description of the world would be frustrat- ing to scientists? The very basis of the scientific approach assumes that nature is underpinned by immutable laws that apply in all places at all times. So this traditional theology sets up an almost unbridgeable chasm between science and religion, one which is often referenced by scientists, and others, as their reason for finding religion insupportable.

By contrast, Joseph Smith's theology, and specifically Joseph Smith's God, is much more in harmony with the scientific approach. We find God existing in nature. We find him described as comprehensible; not that we comprehend him completely now, nor possibly can we while we are in this earthly state, but certainly we expect to comprehend him eventually as we progress to become resurrected beings and on condi- tion that we follow in his footsteps. According to Joseph, not only does God have a perfected, resurrected body, but he is personally endowed with an infinite spirit that shines forth from his person to fill all of space and gives law to all his creations. This spirit is described as the basis for all the laws of nature that science sets as its goal to reveal. The view- point we espouse is that science has yet to discover all of the workings of God's laws (and therefore nature's laws), and that when an unusual event occurs, a healing or an angelic visitation, this is not a supernatural event at all. It is a natural event involving principles of nature that are not yet understood by man, but they are understood by the God of nature who puts them to work for his righteous purposes.

One might rightly ask: if spirit is like light, as described in the previ- ous chapter, and light has a finite speed, how can God be in contact with all his creations instantaneously through his spirit? Wouldn't there be a huge time lag between his command and its execution? We certainly don't know the detailed answer to this question, but here are a couple of interesting points. First, remember that as we learned in the last chapter, while all light is spirit, it does not follow that all spirit is light. There may well be types of spirit that are not constrained by Einstein's rule limiting speeds to the speed of light. Second, scientists are already finding hints that Einstein's rule may be circumvented. For example, current cosmo- logical thinking states that the expansion of space described earlier as a result of the big bang is not limited to the speed of light—and this exception is fundamental to current thinking about the early expansion of the universe after the big bang. In other words, space can be moved faster than the speed of light, even if physical objects can't. Furthermore, there is the possibility of communication through bent (warped) space-time, allowing for possible interstellar short cuts for particles small and big to pass. This idea lies at the heart of most science fiction plots that require interstellar travel in reasonable times. This is not to say that either of these recent discoveries has anything to do with the way God uses spirit to communicate with his creations; rather it simply illustrates that we are already discovering previously unknown phenomena that open the door to communications between points in space that are not limited to the speed of electromagnetic light through normal space. To date, science has opened the door only a crack to some of nature's wonders that might help resolve this question, and surely there are new wonders yet to be discovered. But we digress—let's get back to the question at hand.

Do members of the restored Church believe in miracles or not? Yes, but in our own unique way. We believe that God has the power to make unusual things happen, but not because he sidesteps natural law. Rather he can carry out marvelous acts because he knows all natural law and therefore can work with nature in ways that we can only dream of. When asked how a miracle happens, traditional theology might claim that it is a *mystery*, by which is meant not only that we don't know but also that we can never know because we cannot probe the mind and acts of an inscrutable God. Latter-day Saints don't believe in mysteries in the same way. How a miracle happens may be a mystery, but only in the sense that we have not yet been told how the miracle was performed and what laws of nature were used to make it happen. And this difference in our understanding of miracles results directly from the different way we understand the nature of God.

These ideas are affirmed in the words of apostle John A. Widtsoe, who wrote in his book *Joseph Smith as Scientist*:[1]

- "In Mormon theology, there is no place for immaterialism. . . . Science knows phenomena only as they are associated with matter; Mormonism does the same." (p. 12–13)
- "In [his] conception of God, Joseph Smith was strictly scientific. He departed from the notion that God is a Being foreign to nature and wholly superior to it." (p. 138)

- "A miracle simply means a phenomenon not understood, in its cause and effect relations." (p. 35)

By its own admission, science has uncovered only a small fraction of all there is to discover in the universe. Take dark matter and dark energy as some of the most dramatic recent examples. Clearly we cannot see over the horizon of our current understanding of nature. Every time scientists think we are coming close to understanding most things, new unknowns pop up. There is so much more to discover, it seems we may never run out of new insights.

The teachings of Joseph Smith that God exists in nature while acting as its supreme governor by way of natural law are in perfect harmony with the scientific approach to the world. And as science progresses in its understanding of God's natural law, it does so by his desire to bless his children. Remember that as Brigham Young declared, science is one of the methods by which God endows his children with light, knowledge, and progress, and so Latter-day Saint theology embraces all truth that science can reveal. His quote is worth repeating:

> Every discovery in science and art, that is really true and useful to mankind, has been given by direct revelation from God, though but few acknowledge it. It has been given with a view to prepare the way for the ultimate triumph of truth, and the redemption of the earth from the power of sin and Satan. We should take advantage of all these great discoveries, the accumulated wisdom of ages, and give to our children the benefit of every branch of useful knowledge, to prepare them to step forward and efficiently do their part in the great work.[2]

Notes

1. John A. Widtsoe, *Joseph Smith as Scientist*, General Board Young Men's Improvement Associations, 1908; reprinted by Archive Publishers, 2000.
2. *Journal of Discourses*, Albert Carrington Pub., Liverpool, 1862, **9**, p. 369; Brigham Young discourse, August 31, 1862.

Chapter 8

KNOWLEDGE, TRUTH, AND REASON

The Lord by wisdom hath founded the earth; by understanding hath he established the heavens. By his knowledge the depths are broken up, and the clouds drop down the dew. (Proverbs 3:19–20)

From my early childhood I wanted to be a scientist. I'm not sure why—I guess it sounded exciting to think I might develop some special insights into the fascinating world I saw around me. This desire was reinforced in later years by persistent talk in the media of going to the moon and then seeing Neil Armstrong place his foot on that distant world.

The term *science*, or its linguistic analog, has been around since ancient times. It finds its roots in the Latin word for *knowledge*. It is only in recent times that its usage has narrowed so that when people hear the word *science*, they think of knowledge specifically focused on the natural world. On the other hand, the term *scientist* is of relatively recent origin in the nineteenth century. Before that time, scientists called themselves natural philosophers. I like that latter moniker, because I think it better captures the essence of the role we scientists play. The term *scientist* implies a knower in general, maybe even a kind of know-it-all. But the term *philosopher* derives from Greek and literally means a lover of wisdom. So I think of myself as a natural philosopher, a lover of wisdom about nature.

One of the earliest natural philosophers we know of was the Greek Pythagoras, who lived about 500 BC. We have none of his writings, but instead we have reports of his work from later writers. He apparently had a mystical bent and kept many of his ideas private among his followers. He is famous today among resentful middle school students for his theorem of right triangles, but his impact on modern science is far more profound. He is credited as being the first to declare the important role of mathematics and numbers in describing the natural world. He apparently believed that nature was underpinned by harmonies like those found in musical notes, and by connection mathematics. From his work and that of his followers we derive the term the *music of the spheres*, which has its origins in the idea that the heavenly spheres that housed the planets were related in their sizes and motions to the notes on a musical scale, which in turn were related mathematically.

Twenty-five hundred years after Pythagoras, science has adopted whole-scale the approach of describing nature in mathematical terms. This is true not only for those branches of science we traditionally call natural science (like physics and chemistry) but also for those that deal with the human element of existence (such as social science and political science). The holy grail of virtually every scientific endeavor is to find a way to reduce observations to a mathematical formula. Why? Because numbers are exacting, precise, and well defined. You can test your theory very carefully if you can make a prediction using an equation and then see if the observations match the prediction to the last decimal place. If so, congratulations. If not, congratulations again, because you have found a new unknown, a new question in science which needs addressing—more mysteries to solve!

The search for truth lies at the heart of the scientific endeavor, and in this respect, science shares the same goal as religion. Both are focused on understanding the world without (the natural) and the world within (the human). In Joseph Smith's theology, the search for truth embraces every possible means for finding it, recognizing that the source of all truth is God. For example, in our thirteenth Article of Faith we find: "If there is anything virtuous, lovely, or of good report or praiseworthy, we seek after these things."

What is truth? In Doctrine and Covenants 93 we read, "And truth is knowledge of things as they are, and as they were, and as they are to come" (verse 24). And what is the source of truth? In the same section we read, "The Spirit of truth is of God. I am the Spirit of truth, and John bore record of me, saying: He received a fulness of truth, yea, even of all truth" (verse 26).

We discussed the relationship of truth and light to the spirit of God in a previous chapter, illustrating that this spirit centers in Christ and radiates out from him to fill all his creations. To repeat, in scripture we read, "For the word of the Lord is truth, and whatsoever is truth is light, and whatsoever is light is Spirit, even the Spirit of Jesus Christ." (D&C 84:45) Truth, the knowledge of things as they truly are, is made known through this spiritual light, as it animates our mental faculties.

Knowledge of truth was of vital importance to human eternal development in the mind of Joseph Smith. He declared that this knowledge indeed lies at the heart of what gives God his power:

> In knowledge there is power. God has more power than all other beings, because he has greater knowledge; and hence he knows how to subject all other beings to Him. He has power over all.[1]

So, if we are ultimately to become like God, the pursuit of knowledge should be very high on our list of priorities. And while Joseph maintained that the best way to obtain knowledge of truth was through revelation, he was also a great believer in seeking it out from whatever source was available. For example, very early in the history of the Church, he instituted a School of the Prophets, where not only religious topics were taught, but secular topics as well:

> Teach ye diligently and my grace shall attend you, that you may be instructed more perfectly in theory, in principle, in doctrine, in the law of the gospel, in all things that pertain unto the kingdom of God, that are expedient for you to understand; Of things both in heaven and in the earth, and under the earth; things which have been, things which are, things which must shortly come to pass; things which are at home, things which are abroad; the wars and the perplexities of the nations, and the judgments which are on the land; and a knowledge also of countries and of kingdoms. (D&C 88:78–79)

And despite their poverty and recent expulsion from Missouri, one of the first things Joseph did when the Saints reached Nauvoo was found a university.

In Joseph's mind, not only was knowledge a factor in helping men to become like God, but through revelation, he declared that knowledge had intrinsic value all its own:

If thou shalt ask, thou shalt receive revelation upon revelation, knowledge upon knowledge, that thou mayest know the mysteries and peaceable things—that which bringeth joy, that which bringeth life eternal. (D&C 42:61)

There are many more references in scripture and in the sayings of the prophet Joseph that make it clear that Latter-day Saint theology values highly the gaining of knowledge, not only about those things we would call religious, but everything else as well. This attitude about learning began with Joseph Smith and has carried forward to this day, with the Church investing heavily in the education of its members in schools and universities. The approach finds its impetus in the fundamental doctrine about the nature of God—that he is an exalted man and derives his power from his knowledge of and resulting control over the workings of all nature as administered through his spirit. And it puts Joseph's theology in harmony with science in a way that is quite unique among religions.

One hallmark of science is that its precepts are reasonable. When a new scientific claim is proposed, there is a time-honored way to evaluate it. First, it must conform to all the gathered knowledge, that is, that which comes in the form of careful observations. Second, these observations must be reproducible; that is, if the experiment is redone by a different observer, preferably using a different apparatus, the result must be the same. Third, the new claim must conform to all the scientific principles that are currently well established, or if not, it must present overwhelming evidence that these principles must be reevaluated. The latter review of a scientific claim amounts to requiring it to be *reasonable*. Therefore, it causes consternation among scientists when religion claims the occurrence of miracles because none of these standard methods of evaluating the claim can be met. The observation can't be reproduced and is usually by its very nature out of conformity with known scientific principles. In other words, it is not reasonable.

So, what about miracles? Let's look at these again, this time from a different angle. Can miracles be construed as reasonable? It's true that one of the principal objections to religion is its common belief in the supernatural—that is, in the existence of powers that can override natural law and generate events that are exceptions to natural law. This is a problem that cannot be resolved by strict scientific reasoning alone because science by its very rules of engagement requires that scientifically proven principles be reproducible and that all of the factors that influence the outcome be observable. If you get the same result every time you do the experiment, your result and its associated ideas are validated. And conversely, if you get a different result each time, then your ideas are subject to question or rejection.

And here's the problem: what if you are examining an event that by its very nature is not reproducible, or does not seem so—life, for instance? In more specific terms, we can consider faith healing as an example. One person with cancer has the faith to ask, is given a blessing, and is healed; another with the same cancer has faith to ask, is given a blessing, and dies. A superficial evaluation of this outcome would lead to the conclusion that faith does not heal, that only physiological, biological, and biochemical factors are at play. But what if there is not only faith, but an additional religious parameter at work here which isn't observable, specifically, the will of God. The person of religion would argue that God's will in determining this outcome is even more important than the parameter we earthly observers can observe, namely the faith, and it is the will of God which ultimately determines the outcome of these cases, not the faith alone. The promise is that if we have faith and are healed, our faith has been rewarded by divine intervention, not that everyone who has faith to be healed will be healed. So, with no access to one of the significant factors in determining the outcome (God's will), it is not possible to apply the scientific method to this question. That is because there is an important causal factor at play that we cannot observe, the mind and will of God. But, of course, if we could be mindful of this factor, and hopefully someday we will, we would find the outcome to be perfectly reasonable, not only from a religious perspective, but according to the principles of science as well.

Most religions make no bones about the idea that the workings of a miracle are a mystery, that they are beyond the ability of man to understand their cause. But as explained in the previous chapter, this is not the approach of the restored Church. Our theology describes our relationship with God as intimate—we are his children and have the capacity to become like him in every sense, including his mastery of truth and nature. So that even if we don't currently understand the workings behind seemingly miraculous events, we will understand them someday. Furthermore, we believe that God has given us our ability to think and reason specifically so we can understand him and his ways. Thus, we expect all things to be subject to correct reasoning. It was for this cause that Eliza R. Snow, an intimate confidant of Joseph, penned the words found in one of our most beloved hymns, "O My Father": "Truth is reason, truth eternal tells me I've a Mother there" (*Hymns*, no. 292). Pertinent to our discussion here is her emphasis on the value of reason in determining truth—the ability to reason is a God-given gift to help us identify truth.

The idea that truth, one of the most important divine attributes, is reason affects the way we think about our Heavenly Father and his creations. We expect to be able to understand him and what he reveals to us—if not in this life, then in the next. There are no permanently impenetrable mysteries. God has given us our ability to reason specifically so we can understand all that is true and distinguish between truth and error. So this is how the theology of the restored Church of Christ stands out. Like science, we do expect all things, even those related to the divine, to be reasonable. We may not be able to reason through them perfectly now, but they are reasonable to God, and we expect someday that they will be reasonable also to us when we have become like him and know all that he knows. Not only does all truth fit into one whole, but into one *reasonable* whole. And the reasoning of God is not foreign to our human reasoning, but indeed our human reasoning is a subset of and consistent with that of God, our literal Father.[2]

How do these ideas dovetail with our conceptions of common sense? Does everything that is true and reasonable have to conform to what we could call common sense? As we mentioned earlier, Einstein famously characterized common sense as the collection of prejudices collected by the age of eighteen. Indeed, he was probably the very definition of a person who is willing to call into question common sense. For example, he theorized that gravity is not a force, as Newton had described, but an effect of the warping of four-dimensional space. It certainly doesn't fit into our normal way of thinking, our common sense, that the world is four-dimensional. No one can show you the fourth dimension. Yet his theory about gravity has now gained virtually universal acceptance among reasonable people, and the idea that there are more dimensions than the normal three is now commonplace. If you have questions about this theory you can consult your local physics teacher, and chances are she will be able to explain that in light of lots of indirect evidence, it is reasonable to conclude that there is a fourth dimension even though we can't see it. Not all that is reasonable makes common sense, but given time and a little effort, one can overcome common sense when needed to accommodate reason.

One valuable means to apply reason to any problem is to use the tools of mathematics, which itself is a formal, rigorous method of applying reason and logic to problems. As an example, we started this chapter with mention of the work of Pythagoras in his early attempts to describe nature in terms of numbers and mathematics. These early applications of mathematics to describing the natural world came about as natural philosophers were trying to keep track of and predict the motions of the planets (including the sun and moon) in the heavens. To the ancients, this was critical information, because not only did they keep track of the calendar this way, but since the heavenly bodies were associated with divine powers, their positions were believed to influence events on earth. In the ancient world, there was no distinction made between astronomy and astrology as we make today.

Indeed, it was mathematical logic that brought down the Aristotelian model of the earth-centered universe and replaced it with the Newtonian universe in the eighteenth century. A chink first appeared in the Aristotelian earth-centered model when in the seventeenth century the astronomer Johannes Kepler made very precise measurements of the movements of the planets that showed clearly that they moved in elliptical (oval) orbits around the sun rather than perfect circles around the earth. He used the equations for ellipses and circles to make his point. And finally, when Newton published his work about gravity about a century later, he entitled it *Mathematical Principles of Natural Philosophy*, emphasizing the role that mathematics played in his description of the force of gravity and the motions of objects. He described gravity in the form of an equation that is so powerful in its application that it was used almost three hundred years later to send men to the moon. Since Newton's day, mathematics has become accepted as the most rigorous way to apply reason and logic to any problem.

If truth is reason, and mathematics is one of the best ways to apply reason, does mathematics play any role in theology? The first point to remember is that the Lord has made it clear that all knowledge that is true and reliable comes from him. The second point is that the Lord is drawing back the veil over truth so that in the latter days, his plan is to flood the earth with truth and light:

> A time to come in the which nothing shall be withheld, whether there be one God or many gods, they shall be manifest. All thrones and dominions, principalities and powers, shall be revealed and set forth upon all who have endured valiantly for the gospel of Jesus Christ. And also, if there be bounds set to the heavens or to the seas, or to the dry land, or to the sun, moon, or stars—All the times of their revolutions, all the appointed days, months, and years, and all the days of their days, months, and years, and all their glories, laws, and set times, shall be revealed in the days of the dispensation of the fulness of times. (D&C 121: 28–31)

Given that so much of what the Lord has revealed about nature in these latter days through science is mathematically based, it seems clear that mathematics is one great gift among others he has provided. This may come as an unwelcome thought to those who have struggled through math classes over many years of schooling, and it may stretch the ability of math professors everywhere to remain humble, but I believe that this is true. The power of mathematics to uncover truth is awe-inspiring.

You are probably most familiar with applications of mathematics to create graphs or generate equations to show and describe experimental data. But once experimental data have been reduced to some kind of formula (equation), it is possible to use that equation to predict what the experimental outcomes would be in conditions where the experiment has not yet been performed. A simple example of this involves predicting the weather. After collecting data over many years of atmospheric temperatures and pressures, equations are generated to describe these data; then these equations can be used to predict into the future what the weather will be like—and of course sometimes this works better than others, often to the dismay of picnickers.

In physics and chemistry, we have equations that very accurately predict what particles like atoms, protons, and electrons may do, sometimes according to rules of probability, which is one branch of mathematics. We enjoy the fruits of insights gained using mathematics in our everyday lives: our cars, our TVs, our cell phones, our medicines. One might understandably believe that mathematics is a handy tool that humans have concocted to describe nature, but that the connection between the two is entirely arbitrary and superficial. You might think of mathematics as being like the painting of a person. It's perhaps a good likeness, but the painting in no way captures the entire essence of the person; it's merely a two-dimensional likeness created for our enjoyment. However, let me introduce you to something that happened in 1928 using one of these equations that reveals an uncanny connection between mathematics and the reality of nature.

Do you recall from your school math classes that equations can be solved to give solutions? (I'm sorry if this dredges up nightmare memories, but carry on—it will be worth it.) Some complex equations (and even simple ones) may have more than one solution,[3] and that's all I will say about that. In 1928, an English physicist named Paul Dirac was working with one of the complex equations describing the workings of an electron, when he realized that the equation had two solutions, one representing negative charge, the other representing positive charge. Now Dirac knew like everybody else that electrons have a negative charge, and so he could easily have dismissed that other positive solution to the equation as a mathematical curiosity, nothing more. But not Dirac—he had learned through years of experience to take the relationship between the math describing a phenomenon and the phenomenon itself quite seriously, so he dared to propose that there must be positively charged electrons. Let's be clear: no one had ever observed a positive electron, and most scientists dismissed the claim as absurd. But at least one lab was interested enough to take a look. And, lo and behold, in 1932 they discovered positive electrons, which became known as antielectrons or *positrons*. It was subsequently discovered that there are *anti* particles of all kinds, like protons and neutrons as well, with charge opposite that of the normal particle; and so, antimatter was discovered by mathematics in the human mind before it was ever discovered in nature.

This episode in the history of science does not get much press. But I maintain that it may be one of the most important developments ever. Why? Because it implies that there is a much tighter relationship between mathematics and reality than we ever thought possible. It simply says that the logic of mathematics is so powerful that from it we can deduce the existence of things in nature that we would have no idea were there if we relied on our powers of observation alone. Is it possible then that in general when the math predicts something as yet unobserved (if the math is right), we will find it? This episode, and others like it, implies that nature itself is constructed on mathematical principles, not that math is simply a handy way of describing it. It implies that mathematics may very well be the language of creation itself.

We find a very good analogy to this latter idea in our own humble human endeavors using mathematics. We may design and build in principle a huge, complex skyscraper using mathematical tools, often with the aid of computers; and we do this before a single nail is driven or concrete wall assembled. By the same token, it may be that a universe is created using the tools of logic and reason embedded in mathematical expressions before a single molecule or star is assembled. Such a concept is not incompatible with the multi-stage creation process described in latter-day scripture, as may be found in a careful reading of the Book of Abraham chapter five.

In summary, the theology of Joseph Smith teaches that knowledge, reason, and truth are not only human attributes, but Godly attributes to be sought out and emulated by his children. Our God operates on the same principles of reason and logic as do we, and this because we are of the same family and share a common origin and destiny. We can seek and find truth through reason, acknowledging that these powers are a gift from a Heavenly Father who yearns for our advancement. The search for knowledge through observation, reason, and logic, which informs the scientific endeavor, likewise informs our quest as we seek to become like him. In other words, the scientific approach to truth based on reason and logic is in every respect the approach of Christ's latter-day disciples.

Scientist and apostle John A. Widtsoe aptly stated: "[Joseph Smith] taught doctrines absolutely free from mysticism, and built a system of religion in which the invariable relation of cause and effect is the cornerstone. . . . The Church teaches that all human knowledge and all the laws of nature are part of its religious system."[4]

Amen!

NOTES

1. Joseph Fielding Smith, *Teachings of the Prophet Joseph Smith*, Deseret Book, 1973, p. 288.
2. These concepts are thoroughly developed in John A. Widtsoe, *A Rational Theology as Taught by The Church of Jesus Christ of Latter-Day Saints*, Published for the Use of the Melchizedek Priesthood by the General Priesthood Committee, 1915.
3. For example, the equation $x^2 = 4$ can have two solutions, x = 2 or x = -2.
4. John A. Widtsoe, *Joseph Smith as Scientist*, General Board Young Men's Improvement Associations,1908; reprinted by Archive Publishers, 2000, p. 37.

Chapter 9

FAITH IN RELIGION AND SCIENCE

Who cannot see, that if God framed the worlds by faith, that it is by faith that he exercises power over them, and that faith is the principle of power?[1] *(Lectures on Faith, Lecture First)*

As Latter-day Saints, we say that the very first (most fundamental) principle of the gospel is faith in the Lord Jesus Christ. Why is that? And does faith play any part in science? These are the questions we will address in this chapter.

Let me clarify one important point as we begin: faith is not simply belief. Far from it. Belief is only a minor part of faith; faith is mostly comprised of trust. As a scientist, I like to put numbers on things, so let's estimate that faith is 10 percent belief and 90 percent trust. Those numbers aren't scientific, I just pulled them out of the air to illustrate how much more important trust is to understanding faith than is belief.

An analogy should help. Christ said we need to become like little children. Think back to when you were a child. Did you have faith in your parents? Yes, you did. What did that mean? Well, first of all, it meant that you believed that they existed and that they were your parents—but that really goes without saying. Mostly what it meant was that you trusted in them. First, you trusted that they would be there taking care of you. They were there yesterday, and you expected (trusted) that they would be there again tomorrow—hopefully you had good parents like that. And you trusted that when they told you to do or not to do something that they had a good reason—that they had your best interest at heart. Perhaps they told you not to touch a hot stove, and if you wanted to test their reliability on this point, you touched it. You quickly learned to have faith that they knew what they were talking about. And later in life as a teen, perhaps they demanded that you be home from an evening out with friends at a certain time. If you took them at their word and did so without debate, that demonstrated that you had faith in them. Or, if like many teens you questioned why and weren't particularly keen on their answer, you remembered that hot stove and decided to trust them anyway. You had faith that they knew what they were talking about and acted accordingly. Or maybe you disobeyed and learned by sad experience that nothing good ever happens after midnight.

How does this kind of faith or trust come about? By experience— good and bad. Trust or faith is earned over time. I trust you—I have faith in you now because I've learned through experience that I can rely on you and your word.

Children commonly have explicit faith in their parents. Christ puts himself in the role of parent as the Father of our redemption and exaltation through the power of his Atonement; and he expects us to have faith in him in the same way. The reason that faith is the bedrock foundation of religion is that if we have faith in Christ, we will accept all that he has to offer willingly, including both his gifts (like redemption) and his counsels (like commandments). Without this faith, we would not be motivated to participate in any other aspect of religious life (like repentance or the ordinances of the gospel), nor would we be likely to follow any of God's commandments. Faith must come first, before anything else.

In what ways do we have faith in Christ? First, we have faith (belief) that he exists, that he lived and died for us and was resurrected—but that is just the 10 percent. The other 90 percent of faith involves trusting him. First, we trust that he really can do what he says he will do for us: save us from sin and death and exalt us in his Father's kingdom through the power of his Atonement. Second, we trust that we can rely on his word, today and on into the future. In other words, we trust that we won't wake up one morning and find that he lost his power, or that he has decided to back out on his promises; we trust that he won't say, "I've changed my mind—I'm really not going to save you from the effects of sin and death after all." Third, we have faith that when he asks something of us, like loving our enemies or abstaining from alcohol, that he knows what he is talking about, that he isn't being arbitrary but has a good reason. Fourth, and hardest, we trust that when bad things happen in our lives, as they often do, he will have the power to heal all wounds and mend all broken hearts in the end.

How does faith in Christ come about? The same way faith in anyone comes about—by experience. It usually starts out small in the form of a limited "experiment upon my words" (Alma 32:27). Here's an analogy. Say I am looking for a dentist, and my friend recommends his dentist as caring and capable. At first, I may be skeptical, as we all are about dentists, but I give her a try. The first visit goes well—no blood or shrieking. So I go back again; and as the years go by, I find that my tooth problems are being taken care of, she keeps her appointments, I am being charged reasonable rates, I have a healthy smile, and I actually look forward to my next visit. In the end I trust her to do a good job; I have faith in my dentist. She has withstood the test of time.

In a similar manner, the Lord describes developing faith in him like the growth of a seed, which starts out small but then grows over time into a great bush. Unlike the tiny delicate seed, which can be tossed around or damaged easily, the bush is solid in the ground and able to withstand the strong winds that may arise. We begin by a simple trial, reading scripture or praying. We notice a feeling of peace and hope, and we take further steps. Each step along the way, we find ourselves reaping richer and richer spiritual rewards. At some point, maybe we stumble and feel the resultant loss of stability in our lives, so we learn from this bad experience and return like the prodigal son. As time goes by, we develop a trust that the Lord's promises are real and that we find happiness and contentment only when we draw close to him. Once fully developed, faith in Christ can be rock solid and give us the strength to endure the hardest of hardships. Our trust in him has withstood the test of time.

The word *faith* has come to be used more often in religion than in secular life, but the word applies universally when we have come to trust in any person or thing. As we mentioned in an earlier chapter, science is as heavily reliant on faith as is religion, although most scientists would not use that word. How does science depend on faith?

Faith in Christ and his character undergirds all other aspects of Christian religion. Likewise, there are fundamental principles upon which all science is constructed and in which scientists have implicit faith or trust. Specifically, scientists have faith in the following fundamental (self-evident) truths about nature:

1. What we observe in nature actually exists and isn't a figment of our imagination (as in the movie *The Matrix*). This tenet corresponds to the belief part of faith.
2. There are fundamental laws of nature that underpin all events in nature (as opposed to the ancient belief that events are disconnected from one another and uniquely caused by spirits or gods).
3. The laws of nature operate so that causes of events precede the events themselves.
4. The laws of nature have always been and will always be the same.
5. The laws of nature are the same everywhere in the universe.
6. Scientists deserve to be paid a lot more than they actually get.

I admit that the last one may not be as fundamental as the others, so I'll repent and remove it from the list. The five remaining principles do not derive from the standard methods of science, including observation and making hypotheses to be tested systematically about nature. Instead, these are considered the basic axioms, fundamental truths, or assumptions that science makes about the world. We have faith in these principles because they have stood the test of time; in hundreds of years of observing the world, modern science has never found an instance in nature that contradicts them; on the contrary, we have observed countless instances that reaffirm them. And without a rock-solid faith in these principles, science as we know it would have no meaning, and scientists would not be motivated to seek out nature's laws. Without this faith, we might as well pack up our test tubes and go home.

There is a further way in which faith comes into play in the scientific endeavor. For example, when I teach chemistry students about the laws of thermodynamics (the science related to energy), they often wonder where these laws came from. Specifically, the first law of thermodynamics states that the total energy of the universe is constant—you may remember that one from grade school. To amplify on this, according to Einstein mass and energy are different expressions of the same thing, so this law means really that the total amount of mass (or matter) plus energy (like light and heat) in the universe can't change. So it's a fair question to ask how we know this.

This first law of thermodynamics has been a fundamental principle of science for well over one hundred years and is now taken as absolute truth. But has anyone ever measured the total amount of mass and energy in the universe and then measured it again a few years later to see if it has changed? The answer is no—it's not possible to do, at least not yet. So why do we believe in it? Because we can test it on a limited scale by measuring the mass/energy in systems here on earth. And when we do, we find that the principle is always true about that system no matter the size or type of system we choose. Mass/energy is always conserved—it never disappears into nowhere, and it never appears out of nowhere. Furthermore, this principle has endured the test of time. It was first proposed as a sensible hypothesis based on what we observe from our limited perspective here in the local part of the universe we can see. Then, assuming that the principle applies to the universe as a whole, we derived certain laws that make predictions about local events here on earth for which we could carry out experiments. These measurements confirmed the validity of the local laws, which gave us confidence in the general law about the universe as a whole. Over time, experiments that reinforced this view have accumulated, and no one has ever found a result that refutes it. The first law has stood the test of time, so we have a lot of faith in it, and we exercise that faith every time we carry out an experiment relating to thermodynamics.

This same process to validate a scientific hypothesis has played out for many of the laws of nature in which scientists now have a lot of faith: all the laws of thermodynamics, the laws of quantum mechanics associated with the behavior of photons and tiny particles like electrons, and the law of gravity, to name just a few. These have all withstood the test of repeated experimentation and scrutiny over time, so we have strong faith that they are valid.

You may ask, how do we know these laws are universal, applying in all places at all times? Once again, faith comes into play. As to place, we have lots of evidence that the laws of physics (gravity, light, atomic structure, and so on) apply in all places because the light we receive from distant galaxies and stars behaves exactly as light we receive from within our own solar system. And what is very handy is that the further away the stars and galaxies are, the older the light we perceive from them. That is why long distances in the universe are measured in light years—a light year being the distance (not the time) that light travels in a year, about six trillion miles. So the light we see from a galaxy that is ten billion light years away is ten billion years old—it left that galaxy ten billion years ago. That light carries with it a lot of information about the structure and functioning of the materials in those distant stars a long time ago. And we can see from that light that once again the same laws applied when the light left that galaxy as apply today here. These results reinforce our faith in the fundamental assumptions listed above upon which all science is based: namely that these scientific laws and principles are universal in both place and time. If we are to be honest, the answer to the question *How do we know?* is that we don't really. We have very strong confidence (faith) that things are as we believe, but we hold open the possibility that with new observations, we might have to change our minds.

Indeed, we have had to change our minds repeatedly in science. Take for example Newton's law of gravity discussed in an earlier chapter. This model of gravity held sway for two hundred years after Newton, by which time it had become accepted as almost unassailable. But assailed it was by another genius, Albert Einstein.

Newton had described gravity as an invisible force that reached out from one body (like the earth) to another (like the moon) and pulled them together. This idea was hard for people to accept at the time—what exactly was this force which could reach across empty space but had no material presence? It seemed like magic. Yet the model worked so well in describing the motions not only of heavenly bodies but of cannon balls and everything else, that people soon accepted the idea of the force of gravity without worrying about what the force actually was. They took it on faith that such a force must be real even though you couldn't observe it and had no idea what it was.

A chink appeared in Newton's model when it could not account for small deviations in the orbit of the planet Mercury. This problem may sound trivial, but precise measurements such as those mentioned here are key to testing scientific ideas, and the small discrepancy led to a new insight. Specifically, with his world-class imagination, Einstein envisioned that if the world held a fourth dimension, the effects that we attribute to gravity, like the motions of the planets or the falling of an apple, could be accounted for by the warping of four-dimensional space. The best way to envision this bizarre concept is to imagine what life would be like if we were two-dimensional creatures living in a two-dimensional world. It would be as if we were paper cutouts moving about on a table-top. As citizens of this flat world, we would assume that our world was perfectly flat. But what if, unbeknownst to us, our flat world (our table top) were curved into an unseen third dimension. Then as objects moved on the tabletop, they would seem to be drawn toward each other as they moved in curvy paths, and we would be tempted to think there was a force pulling on them. To be more specific, let's imagine that the table-top is flexible like a trampoline fabric, and that whenever a heavy object sits on it, it causes the fabric to sag in that spot. Objects that come near the sag would always move as if they were being *pulled* toward the other object. And if they were already moving sideways when they got near the object, they would appear to spiral in. Perhaps you've seen this idea in action at an amusement park, where you put a penny into a funnel-like contraption and you can watch the penny spiral downwards into the hole—same idea. And there goes your penny!

Now, so that we can use this analogy to help us envision a fourth dimension, imagine that we add a dimension to our two-dimensional analogy so that we come close to understanding Einstein's model of gravity in the world we actually live in. We can do a thought experiment as Einstein did. The tabletop converts into the three-dimensional space we live in. Every object with weight then warps the 3D space into an unseen fourth dimension, and as other objects come close, they seem to move toward the first object as if they were attracted to it. But they're not attracted—they are simply moving in what seems to be a straight line through curved space.

This model sounds bizarre; after all, who has ever seen the fourth dimension? Like most physics models, it is based on sophisticated math that mercifully does not belong in our discussion. At first, many physi-cists were skeptical. But the strength of the model lies in the fact that it fixed the problem with the orbit of Mercury. And this new model received a strong vote of confidence when it was shown that even light (which has no mass) follows a curved path around a very heavy object like our sun (as if it did have mass), something Newton's model could not explain. Space is apparently not just nothing. It is a thing that can be distorted (warped) by the presence of matter into a fourth dimension.

Whether you follow this logic or not, here's the point. No one has ever directly experienced this fourth dimension proposed in Einstein's model. Yet scientists have a high degree of faith that it exists. This is because it is the only way up to now that we can explain the curvature in the path of light around heavy objects.

The existence of other dimensions isn't the only recent claim that science makes requiring a good deal of faith. Prime examples that have appeared in the last few years include the existence of dark matter and dark energy, which we discussed in previous chapters. Scientists now believe that these two kinds of things make up 95 percent of the universe, but we can't see, hear, taste, smell, or touch them, and none of our machines can detect them. Yet many scientists believe in them. Now that's faith!

I have repeatedly used the word *model* to refer to the way scientists describe the natural world. This term has a very specific meaning in science that is pertinent to our discussion here. Science makes an effort to describe real things and events in nature by creating models. A model is a mental representation (often expressed in mathematical terms) of a natural phenomenon but it is not the phenomenon itself. In this respect, a scientific model is always somewhat limited.

Again, an analogy can help illustrate this principle. Imagine that you are trying to describe a platypus to someone who has never seen or heard of a platypus. You would probably try to help your friend develop a mental image of the animal by saying that it has a beak like a duck, a tail like a beaver, has fur and swims like an otter, lays eggs like a bird, and so on. And in fact, when explorers first encountered the platypus in Australia they sent word back to England of this very sort to describe the animal. They were creating a model of the platypus by referring to things familiar to the reader. And subsequently when they sent a platypus back to England, the animal arrived in such a poor state of preservation that people thought it must be a hoax; that someone had cobbled together parts of different animals—ha ha!

Scientific models often work on the same basis. We find ourselves trying to describe something we can't observe or experience directly by analogy to things that are familiar. For example, for centuries there was a debate over whether light was a wave or a particle. Perhaps it behaves like sound, and therefore a wave—but the question arises: a wave in what, given that it is passing through empty space? Or perhaps it behaves like a bullet—but how can it have no mass? In both cases, the proposed model falls short because it leaves a question unanswered. In the end, we have settled on a compromise, and we consider light a *particle-wave*. But what does that mean? Does it make any real sense? The math works really well in predicting the behavior of light, but the question remains: Does light have to be a particle or a wave at all? Does the math for this modern model capture the actual essence of light in every respect?

The reality is that light is light. It doesn't have to be a particle or a wave. It can be a thing entirely unique in itself. But under different circumstances, for our convenience, we can model it as a particle or a wave as we wish in order to satisfy our current need—perhaps to explain our most recent experimental results or to predict what a certain beam of light will do. We do this because particles and waves are familiar to us. But that doesn't mean that light is the model, that is, a particle, a wave, or even a particle-wave, any more than a platypus is a duck or a beaver, or even a duck-beaver!

Thus, when Einstein proposes a four-dimensional model of the universe to explain gravity, he is presenting an argument to explain an aspect of the world that we can't directly experience in terms that we are familiar with—dimensions. We are used to the idea of three dimensions, and we can imagine a possible fourth dimension. But we have to exercise faith that the world can be described that way; and yet maybe it really is that way, or maybe it isn't.

Scientists maintain a very strong faith in the five self-evident truths about nature listed above, but they have limited faith in their models only so far as they work to explain all observations. Thus they keep an open mind to the prospect that if new observations require that a model be revised or replaced, they are ready to do so. That happened to Newton's model of gravity; it may happen to Einstein's someday.

The scientific endeavor involves seeking new insights, and then embracing them once proven. This is not to say, however, that changes come easily and without controversy. The more radical the change, the more skeptical the scientific community and the more resistance. Extraordinary claims require extraordinary proofs.[2] But one of the great strengths of the scientific process is its flexibility and the ability to embrace new truths as they are revealed.

By the same token, in religion we maintain a solid faith in Christ and his Atonement as a fundamental principle, but we try to keep an open mind when it comes to other doctrines for which a fulness of truth may not as yet have been revealed. As in science, truth in religion is meted out carefully by the Lord, as he provides "here a little and there a little." (2 Nephi 28:30) It is interesting that he has reserved the revelation of so much of his truth for the last days, and that these truths are made known to his children both through revelation and through science, as Brigham Young taught. Just as in science, sometimes when new truths are revealed in the religious realm through revelation, they challenge past traditions of faith. Certainly there is no one in modern times who was more inclined to challenge religious traditions than Joseph Smith. He said on one occasion:

> I have tried for a number of years to get the minds of the Saints prepared to receive the things of God; but we frequently see some of them, after suffering all they have for the work of God, will fly to pieces like glass as soon as anything comes that is contrary to their traditions: they cannot stand the fire at all. How many will be able to abide a celestial law, and go through and receive their exaltation, I am unable to say, as many are called, but few are chosen.[3]

And on another occasion, only a year before his death, Joseph lamented:

> I could explain a hundred fold more than I ever have of the glories of the kingdoms manifested to me in the vision, were I permitted, and were the people prepared to receive them.[4]

I often wonder if we are any more prepared to receive new revelation that may fly in the face of our traditions than were the saints in Joseph's day.

In the twenty-first century, are people inclined to look to God for answers about the world as Joseph Smith was? How about scientists? It is commonly thought that almost all scientists are godless atheists, but you may be surprised at how many scientists are believers at one level or another. A Pew research study in 2009 showed that among members of the American Association for the Advancement of Science, the world's largest general science organization, 51 percent claimed a belief in God or a higher power.[5] Many scientists recognize that the order we observe in nature must have a rational source.

The quest among members of the restored Church for truth shares many characteristics in common with science, not the least of which is the exercise of faith as one of its foundational operating principles: faith in Christ for Latter-day Saints and other Christians; faith in the fundamentals of nature for science. From the viewpoint of a Latter-day Saint scientist, faith in nature really constitutes faith in Christ as the law-giver of nature; and in our reliance on faith as a working principle, we share a major point of agreement with scientists everywhere.

NOTES

1. *Lectures on Faith*, Lecture 1, verse 17. These are lectures given at the School of the Prophets in Kirtland, Ohio, in the winter of 1834–35. They were prepared for publication by Joseph Smith and printed in the original *Doctrine and Covenants* and subsequent reprintings until 1921. The full text is found online and has also been reprinted several times over the years.
2. A favorite saying of astronomer Carl Sagan in both his writings and in the television series *Cosmos*, Digitally Remastered Disc Collector's Edition, Cosmos Studios Inc., 2000.
3. Joseph Smith, *History of the Church*, B. H. Roberts, ed., Deseret Book, 2nd ed., 1971, **6**, p. 185.
4. Joseph Fielding Smith, *Teachings of the Prophet Joseph Smith*, Deseret Book, 1973, p. 305.
5. Pew Research Center, Religion and Public Life: http://www.pewforum. org/2009/11/05/scientists-and-belief.

Chapter 10

COSMOS AND CHAOS

These things I have spoken unto you, that in me ye might have peace. In the world ye shall have tribulation: but be of good cheer; I have overcome the world. (John 16:33)

The ancient Egyptians viewed the world as a continuing struggle between the powers of order, law, truth, harmony, and justice on the one hand, and decay, evil, and destruction on the other. As was common practice in these ancient civilizations, these forces were personified in the form of gods. The goddess of order and harmony was Ma'at, and she was depicted in art with the ostrich feather of truth in her headdress. In fact, her name literally meant truth. Her feather played an important part in the final judgment of the soul after death, as each individual's heart was weighed on a scale against the feather. If the heart was lighter than the feather, this showed that the person was just and good, and worthy of eternal life; if the heart was heavier, the person was deemed evil and condemned to be consumed by a horrible monster. The idea of Ma'at has carried forward even to our day, as we see statues of Lady Justice on our courthouses, blindfolded and with a scale in her hand.

To the Egyptians, in opposition to Ma'at was Isfet. Isfet represented the forces that worked against Ma'at, the forces that would tear down and destroy all that is good in the world. The Pharaoh's responsibility was to counterbalance the influence of Isfet in favor of Ma'at, and ideally a balance could be struck between these two opposing forces to achieve harmony in the universe. Both forces were essential to maintaining this balance, and each served to highlight the role of the other.

It is not surprising that this concept of a balance between the forces of good and those of evil are reflected in the teachings of Lehi in the Book of Mormon, given the strong influence of Egyptian culture on the neighboring people of Israel in his day. Conversely, it may well be said that the Hebrews had a significant impact on Egyptian theology much earlier through Abraham and Joseph and that these fundamental principles of religious thought were shared by both cultures as a result. Lehi teaches the following to his son Jacob:

> For it must needs be, that there is an opposition in all things. If not so, my firstborn in the wilderness, righteousness could not be brought to pass, neither wickedness, neither holiness nor misery, neither good nor bad. Wherefore, all things must needs be a compound in one; wherefore, if it should be one body it must needs remain as dead, having no life neither death, nor corruption nor incorruption, happiness nor misery, neither sense nor insensibility. (2 Nephi 2:11)

Here again, the world is depicted as an ongoing struggle between the forces that would bring order and goodness versus those that would bring disorder and evil. The contrast between these forces is essential to all existence, and it is the role and right of every individual to choose between the two and be judged accordingly. Of course, the significant difference between the Egyptian picture and that of Christianity is the imposition of Christ into the process, whereby he can tip the scales in favor of goodness through the power of the Atonement if the individual chooses to accept the gift along with its provisions.

The struggle between good and evil is a common theme among religions throughout history and has permeated human thought since it was first revealed to Adam and Eve that they had a choice to make in the garden. Among the ancient Greeks, Pythagoras (~500 BC) was the first to give the name *cosmos* to the orderly universe with its basis in mathematics. Many of the Greek philosophers taught that the order of the universe was preceded by chaos, a state of disorder or non-being, which contrasted with the order that came after.

In modern times, the terms cosmos and chaos have taken on more distinct notions of opposites along the lines of Ma'at and Isfet, cosmos representing the orderly, law-abiding universe, and chaos a state of disorder and lawlessness. This duality was given new life in the nineteenth century with the development of a branch of physics and chemistry called thermodynamics. That's a big word, but it simply represents the field of scientific study dealing with heat and energy in general. I'm going to take you on a short journey into the world of thermodynamics, but don't worry—it'll be fun, and there's no final exam at the end.

We've already mentioned the first law of thermodynamics, familiar to all who have taken high school science, although not necessarily by that name. It states that the total amount of energy (including matter, which is a condensed form of energy) in the universe is constant. This is sometimes worded, "energy is neither created nor destroyed but can change from one form to another," like the energy of motion of your car being converted into heat in the brake pads when you step on the brakes.

There is another law of thermodynamics that is a little more esoteric and therefore less talked about over the dinner table or in school. This second law has profound connections to the ancient Egyptian beliefs about Ma'at and Isfet, and the teachings in the Book of Mormon about opposition in all things. The law states that every event that occurs in nature increases the amount of disorder in the universe. As you are well aware, scientists generally disdain to use common words in their work— it's a lot more fun to invent new ones, and besides, this maintains the aura of mystery about science. Thus, we have taken to calling the disorder in nature *entropy*. So, the *second law of thermodynamics* states that every event that occurs in nature causes the entropy of the universe to increase. Let's consider the implications of this law.

No doubt you have noticed that the natural tendency of things is to run down. Over time, your car turns into a rattletrap, your aging body weakens, your silverware tarnishes. Even those stars in the heavens that seem eternal eventually run out of fuel and die. All this is in part because everything you encounter in the world around you is made up of tiny atoms. Each of these has independent motion, and while you may be able to herd most of them to do what you want, there will always be a percentage of them that go their own way. Take your precious dream car for example. You worked hard to save up and buy it, so you want it to stay perfect forever. But no matter how careful you are, as you drive it, the motion and heat in the engine and the shaking from bumps in the road will gradually wear away and loosen the metal joints; rattles start to appear, the engine becomes less efficient, and the brakes need replacing. Even if you just put the car in your garage and never drive it, metal parts will start to rust, plastic parts will become brittle—your dream car won't be such a dream anymore.

This all sounds rather depressing, and sometimes things can be that way, but why does this turn into a scientific law that applies to EVERYTHING in the universe? Surely some things get better and more ordered with time—it isn't all bad! Let's dig a little deeper.

We say that very orderly systems of atoms are low entropy (low disorder). A solid material, like a lump of coal, is a good example. The atoms are pretty much locked in place and can't move around randomly—hence low disorder. Conversely, we say that very disorderly systems of atoms are high entropy (high disorder). An example is a gas in which the atoms are far apart and bouncing around like popcorn in a popcorn popper.

The whole field of thermodynamics got its impetus from efforts to understand the workings of steam engines in the early days of the industrial revolution. Early steam engines were very inefficient (and dangerous!), and the goal was to improve their performance and lower the mortality rate. These engines make use of the energy locked up in a fuel like coal, in which the atoms have low entropy (disorder). The goal of every engine that works on the basis of heating up gases (like steam in a steam engine or combustion gases in a gasoline engine) is to convert heat energy from burning a fuel, like coal, into the energy of motion of a machine, like a locomotive. To be clear, heat energy is also a type of energy of motion—the random motion of the atoms in the gas. And the hotter the gas, the more random and chaotic the motion of the atoms (and therefore the higher the entropy). So, in fact, what a steam engine does is first to convert the low-disorder energy locked in the coal into high-disorder energy in the steam; then it converts the chaotic (high-disorder) motion of the atoms in the steam into the orderly motion of the atoms in the locomotive all moving down the railroad track in the same direction at the same speed. This orderly locomotive motion would result from the orderly motion of the atoms in the engine's piston, all moving together in orderly fashion to push on the locomotive.

This is not easy to do. The atoms in the steam in the cylinder above the piston are moving every which way. Only those steam atoms that are moving in such a way as to strike the top of the piston and push the piston down in the engine contribute to the motion of the piston and therefore of the locomotive. The energy of the rest of the steam atoms (that are going the other way and therefore don't push down on the piston) is wasted—it goes toward heating up the metal in the locomotive and the air around it. This wasted heat is what causes the entropy (disorder) of the surroundings, and therefore of the universe overall to increase. When this heat is transferred out to the air, it causes the air atoms to move even more chaotically than before as the temperature rises. The resulting disorder in the air molecules cannot be undone—the entropy of that part of the universe increases for good because the order that was in the coal is now lost to the disorder in the air and can't be recovered.

In a nutshell, the order of the atoms in the coal that burned in the locomotive has now been transformed into two kinds of motion: the orderly motion of the atoms in the locomotive moving down the track, and the chaotic motion of atoms in the heated air. In the latter case, the order that was in that portion of the atoms of the coal has been lost forever. When you measure the difference between the amount of order in the locomotive moving down the track versus the amount of disorder in the heated engine and air and compare that to the order that was in the coal in the first place, the resulting disorder is always greater. More of the order in the original coal has been converted to disorder than to order in the process. The entropy (disorder) of the universe has increased overall.

It turns out that when scientists look at any naturally occurring event, that is, whenever energy changes hands as it must for anything to happen, some orderly atomic motion is lost to disorder. Nature is not being consciously malicious when operating this way. It is simply playing the odds.

Here's another way of thinking about it. Consider what arrangements of atoms you would consider *orderly*. For instance, think of a hundred atoms in a box that is much bigger than their total volume, so that they can easily move around. They are free to go anywhere they want. Which patterns would you consider *ordered*? Maybe all of the atoms bunched together in one corner? Or all of them evenly spaced throughout the box and sitting motionless? There may be many patterns you would consider ordered. But I think you can imagine that there are infinitely more patterns that you would consider *disordered*, especially if the atoms are in motion. Nature doesn't consider any one of these patterns any more likely than any other, so making a distinction between ordered and disordered is really a matter of personal choice on your part. Disordered systems are always more numerous than ordered ones, so disordered ones are just more likely to occur.

That is why natural events always tend toward greater disorder or greater entropy. And that is why your car turns into a rattletrap. The ordering of atoms in your new car is just one of an infinite variety of ways to arrange the car's atoms, and there are a lot more of those arrangements that fall into the rattletrap category.

As events occur and the entropy of the universe increases, so the universe is essentially running down like a wound-up clock. Eventually, there won't be any more order in the universe at all. Chaos will prevail. No more stars, planets, galaxies, pizza—all gone. All that will be left will be a thin haze of atoms spread through space doing nothing interesting. This is the so-called *heat death* predicted for the universe by the second law, trillions of years hence. To quote T. S. Eliot, "This is the way the world ends, not with a bang but a whimper." [1]

You now have a grasp of the second law of thermodynamics. So you are ready to ask the question: if the arrow of time is always directed toward decay, how then is it possible for things to sometimes get more ordered? After all, stars and planets are being created, wolf cubs are born, acorns turn into oak trees. And here's the answer: the second law doesn't say that all things within the universe devolve toward chaos, only that the universe as a whole increases in entropy every time a wolf cub is born. Consider that for a wolf cub to be born, the mother must kill many other animals (destroying their order) over the period of a pregnancy, and a good portion of that food energy is not used to nourish the fetus but is eliminated as waste or expended as heat to keep the mother warm. If you balance the amount of energy that goes into creation of the cub (or anything else), it is outweighed (and it always is) by the amount of energy that is lost to disorder, to waste or to heat, in making it. So, the second law does not in any way prohibit the creation of order in any small (local) system like a wolf cub; it simply states that when order is created, an even greater amount of disorder is generated. For creation to be achieved, an even greater measure of destruction is required in nature.

So what does this have to do with Ma'at and with Lehi? Perhaps that is obvious. Modern science echoes and affirms the teaching that there are opposing forces in nature—creation and destruction, order and disorder, cosmos and chaos—and that the forces of creation and order must battle against the natural tendency for things to become disordered. It is one of the most fundamental truths in all of creation, as taught in Joseph Smith's theology and in one of the most firmly established principles of modern science. Creation can't be achieved without destruction in science. Goodness cannot be achieved except there be evil in theology. The two concepts coincide.

Further light is cast upon this subject in the teachings of King Benjamin:

> For the natural man is an enemy to God, and has been from the fall of Adam, and will be, forever and ever, unless he yields to the enticings of the Holy Spirit, and putteth off the natural man and becometh a saint through the atonement of Christ the Lord, and becometh as a child, submissive, meek, humble, patient, full of love, willing to submit to all things which the Lord seeth fit to inflict upon him, even as a child doth submit to his father. (Mosiah 3:19)

Clearly, as participants in nature, human beings are as susceptible to the workings of the second law of thermodynamics as everything else. Our physical selves and actions are by nature more prone to favor the forces of chaos than those of cosmos, the forces of destruction over the forces of creation. It takes an extra measure of power to fulfill the requirements to be a saint (the champion of order) and to overcome the natural man (the champion of disorder). That power comes by way of the spirit of God, which, when infused into the equation, can overwhelm the powers of entropy (chaos) that pull us down. And this is the great gift that Christ has offered us, that through his Atonement he has "overcome the world" (John 16:33) in that he has the power to overwhelm the forces of darkness and destruction that dominate the natural world as reflected in the second law. He has the power to reverse the natural process of death, both physical death and spiritual death. He has the power to lift us up beyond the reach of the second law into a plane of existence that allows not only for the absence of chaos in our lives, but to an eternal endowment of cosmos, of Ma'at, of creative power. And that is one way of understanding the great message, the good news of the gospel. It takes on profound new insight when seen in the light of the laws of thermodynamics.

Having said all this, it is important to recognize that these principles of thermodynamics were not known in Joseph Smith's day. This law, and its interpretation in terms of the atomic nature of matter, was developed in Europe during the latter half of the nineteenth century long after

Joseph's death. Yet, in this respect, Joseph's theology and science find common ground—their teachings are complementary. Furthermore, the clear expression of the doctrine of opposition in all things in the Book of Mormon is one unique aspect of Joseph Smith's view of Christian theology. It is unique in the sense that Joseph's vision of the universe encompasses a heaven and heavenly beings not divorced from the dichotomy of cosmos and chaos but operating always in concert with the struggle between these opposing primal forces. It affirms the essential role of opposites in creation and resolves the dilemma of evil in the world. We will delve further into this principle as it relates to modern science, free will, and human accountability in our next chapter.

NOTE

1.   From T. S. Eliot's poem "The Hollow Men," found in numerous publications and online, for example at https://www.shmoop.com/hollow-men/poem -text.html.

Chapter 11

OPPOSITION AND FREE WILL

And I, God, divided the light from the darkness. And I, God, called the light Day; and the darkness, I called Night. (Moses 2:4,5)

As discussed in the previous chapter, in the Book of Mormon we are taught that there must be opposition in all things. Specifically, according to Lehi's teaching:

> For it must needs be, that there is an opposition in all things. If not so, my firstborn in the wilderness, righteousness could not be brought to pass, neither wickedness, neither holiness nor misery, neither good nor bad. (2 Nephi 2:11)

We generally think of this opposition in terms of the opposites of good and evil, creation and destruction, cosmos and chaos. But Lehi goes on:

> And if ye shall say there is no law, ye shall also say there is no sin. If ye shall say there is no sin, ye shall also say there is no righteousness. And if there be no righteousness there be no happiness. And if there be no righteousness nor happiness there be no punishment nor misery. And if these things are not there is no God. And if there is no God we are not, neither the earth; for there could have been no creation of things, neither to act nor to be acted upon; wherefore, all things must have vanished away. And now, my sons, I speak unto you these things for your profit and learning; for there is a God, and he hath created all things, both the heavens and the earth, and all things that in

them are, both things to act and things to be acted upon. And
to bring about his eternal purposes in the end of man, after he
had created our first parents, and the beasts of the field and the
fowls of the air, and in fine, all things which are created, it must
needs be that there was an opposition; even the forbidden fruit
in opposition to the tree of life; the one being sweet and the
other bitter.

Wherefore, the Lord God gave unto man that he should
act for himself. Wherefore, man could not act for himself save
it should be that he was enticed by the one or the other. (2 Ne
2:13–16)

Clearly the principle of opposition applies broadly among God's creations and is an eternal principle upon which our very existence is based.
Yet while the contrast between good and evil is a common theme among
Christian religions, the Latter-day Saint viewpoint goes beyond what
is normally taught. For others, the perfect goodness of a God outside
nature generates a dilemma, for an underlying principle in traditional
Christian theology is that God created the universe from nothing and
created each man and woman initially and completely at birth. Thus, the
question arises: how could a perfectly good God intentionally create evil
in the world and in man? This question has vexed Christian theologians
for two thousand years, and endless sophistry has been expended trying
to answer it.

By contrast, Joseph Smith solves this problem neatly when he
declares: "The mind or the intelligence which man possesses is co-equal
with God himself," and Joseph Fielding Smith clarifies that by "co-
equal" Joseph means *co-eternal*. [1] Thus, his theology teaches that each
person has always existed in some form and thus can act independent of
God's will. Man cannot point to a primal creator as responsible for his
choices. We cannot blame God for our imperfect choices, for while he
has added abundantly to the measure of our existence with both a life in
the spirit world and in this one, he has done so by adding measure to a
self that was already existent. Furthermore, according to Lehi's teaching,
good and evil have always existed and are part of the underlying fabric
of the universe, as fundamental to the universe as time and matter themselves. God exists, and we exist, only because the opposites he describes
are at play. And if the purpose of mankind is to have joy, this can only

come about in a universe in which "if they never should have bitter, they could not know the sweet." (D&C 29:39)

Indeed, in the creation story itself we learn of several opposites or contrasting alternatives, and in part the act of creation is presented as the process of separating these alternatives so that the one may be understood in contrast to the other.

- Light and dark
- Water on the earth and water above the earth
- The tree of life and tree of knowledge of good and evil
- Seas and dry land
- Daytime and night time
- Sun and moon
- Plants and animals
- Animals in the sea and animals on the land
- Male and female (gender)
- Man and woman
- To eat of the fruit or not
- Life and death

We don't think about it much in these terms, but the principle of opposition is extremely important in allowing us to perceive and understand the world around us. How would we be able to see anything if there were no opposing light and dark in the world?

This idea is well understood among artists. When you were a child, and you doodled with your watercolor paint set or your crayons, you were intent on making your masterpiece interesting by choosing lots of different colors. The fancy term for color in art is hue; but artists realize that there is another aspect of painting that is often even more important in bringing out the subject against the background—and that is value. Value has to do with how dark or light your color is. If you are painting a brown horse against a green tree and all the colors have the same value, the horse won't stand out very well. It's important that the horse and the tree differ not only in color but in value as well. An extreme example of this concept is the subject of an art joke: an artist hangs a completely white canvas on the museum wall with the caption "White cow in a snow storm."

In the opposite extreme is the Renaissance painter Caravaggio, who was famous for his chiaroscuro technique with strong contrasts in value that made for a very dramatic scene and brought the subjects into clear focus. In art, the stronger the contrast in value (what we might call opposition), the easier it is to see the subject. And in life, the sharper the contrast in value between good and evil, and other opposites we encounter, the easier it is to distinguish between the two.

The principle of opposition relies on the existence of options or pairs of alternatives. Where there are contrasting alternatives, there is choice. And only where choice between alternatives is available can there be freedom of choice, or in other words *agency*. Where the alternatives have moral character, we call this agency *moral agency*.

When you think about it, this principle of opposition and its corollary agency applies in virtually all fields. It is in the contrasts between alternatives that things most often become clear to us. This is what Lehi taught, and it is as true in temporal matters as it is in spiritual, as well on earth as it is in heaven.

It is no wonder then that the principle of opposition applies broadly also in science. Think back on your science classes from school. You can probably remember many scientific principles that come in opposite or complementary pairs. Here are a few:

- Positive and negative charges, as on protons and electrons
- North and south poles on magnets
- Cold objects versus hot objects
- Male and female genders in biology
- The presence of a vacuum versus the presence of matter
- Left-handed molecules versus right-handed molecules
- Living matter versus inanimate matter
- Passing or failing your chemistry class

The ancient natural philosophers also thought of nature in terms of complementary pairs. In fact, in the fifth century BC, Aristotle attempted to organize the understanding of the four material elements they described here on earth (air, water, earth, and fire) in terms of opposite characteristics, wet versus dry and hot versus cold. Air was considered a combination of hot and wet; earth a combination of cold and dry, and so forth. However, these ancient scientists did not hold that vacuum and matter were opposites. Aristotle insisted that a vacuum was not possible, that nature filled all of space with something. Hence the familiar saying "Nature abhors a vacuum." In consequence, to the majority of ancient thinkers, matter was infinitely divisible. You could keep dividing a piece of gold forever in half, and you would still have gold, although not even enough to buy a peanut. You could never get to the point where there was no gold—that would be a vacuum. But that's not how we envision the world today. Instead, we think of individual atoms set in stark contrast (or opposition) to the empty space in between.

As we consider the atom, we enter the realm in modern physics, which is described by a special branch of science called *quantum mechanics*, introduced in a previous chapter. You will recall (I hope) that this science is based on the simple idea that some things come in indivisible units, like letter grades in a physics class or people. You're probably aware that there is no space on the census record for fractions! So, for example, you can't divide up a helium atom into smaller parts and still have a helium atom. Helium atoms, and all their brethren atoms, come in units of one atom, two atoms, three atoms, and so on. It is the same for the individual protons, neutrons, and electrons that make up atoms. They in turn come in units—you either have an electron or you don't. We say that atoms and electrons are *quantized*.

What is even more interesting, and far less intuitive, is that the energies these tiny particles can have are also quantized. This idea is a little deep scientifically but may be familiar to you from your past science classes. If not, give it a try. According to quantum theory, as it dances around the nucleus of the helium atom, an electron may have *this* specific higher energy, or *that* specific lower energy, but it may not have any energy in between. When an electron in the atom jumps *down* in energy from *this* to *that*, it gives off a photon of light, and the energy of that photon is equal to the difference in energy between *this* and *that*. The helium atom can't produce a photon of any old energy, only a photon of the energy corresponding to the difference between *this* and *that*. And that's that! You may be interested to know that this rule of quantum mechanics is what allows us to say that a star millions of light years from earth contains the same kind of helium atoms we have here on earth—because we see in the light from that star photons that only helium can produce because of its unique electron energies.

You see that atomic energies and photons are participants in the universal game of alternatives in all things without which nature could not function. There are choices to be made between alternatives even for electrons. The electron must be in one energy state or the other (*this* or *that*), but not in between. Does the electron consciously choose between these alternative energies? This is a philosophical question we won't get into here. The point is that even at the most fundamental level, nature functions on the basis of alternatives.

But let's not be too hasty in dismissing the possibility that even humble electrons might have choices to make. There exists a well-established principle in physics called the *Heisenberg uncertainty principle*. Put succinctly, it states that for very small particles like electrons, we can't be sure exactly where they are at any moment and/or what motions they are engaged in. Hence *uncertainty*. This concept is part of quantum mechanics, and its acceptance into scientific thought in the early twentieth century completely undermined the long-held belief that we could accurately predict the behavior of all objects—remember Newton's idea of a mechanical universe. Electrons are not like bullets, which you can track accurately and predict where they will hit on the target. Rather, if you fire an electron at a detector in a certain type of experiment, it may end up where you would predict as if it were a bullet, or it may hit the detector to the left or to the right. You can't know. And it's not that you can't know because you don't know how, but rather it is a fundamental law of nature that the point where the electron lands *cannot* be known. It's as if the electron gets to choose. Spooky but true, at least by our current understanding.

As I mentioned, ever since the days of Newton in the eighteenth century, it was a strongly held belief among scientists that the universe could be described as a machine. This was long before the uncertainty found in quantum mechanics had been discovered. To scientists in this earlier day, in theory if you knew the equations that described the movements of all the parts of the universe-machine, then in principle it should be possible to predict exactly what every object in the universe, including people, would do on into the indefinite future. This point of view raised all kinds of interesting philosophical questions leading to a kind of deterministic attitude about life. How could there be free will if everything could be predicted by complex mathematics? In Joseph Smith's day, this is what educated people believed, and it presented a problem—it robbed many people of faith in religion, or at least their faith in human free will and accountability. It is noteworthy, therefore, that the Book of Mormon and Joseph Smith take a stand in favor of free will, going against the then-current scientific view.

But in the twentieth century, science learned more and changed its mind. With the advent of quantum mechanics and its notion of uncertainty at the subatomic level, the possibility of free will opens right back up. If human thought processes occur in the brain by means of electrical impulses, at the root of which is the behavior of electrons in atoms, then there is uncertainty involved. You can't be certain what tiny particles like electrons will do, due to the uncertainty principle. Suddenly science and religion are no longer at odds: our every decision is not predetermined, cannot be predicted. We can choose whether or not to sleep in on Saturday knowing that our choice was not predetermined from the beginning of time. We can choose to love or hate our neighbor, not because the motions of our atoms led us to an inevitable mechanical conclusion, but freely. In this respect, the restored Church and science have found common ground with a tip of the hat to free will, leaving us responsible in the end for the actions we pursue. And in science, with the advent of the Heisenberg uncertainty principle in the twentieth century, one is left with the question *If choice is not predetermined by physics, how then does it come about?* Science has no answer, so we have to turn to religion and the possibility of a world apart from that which the eye can see.

On a very practical level, we have come to rely on the scientific principle of contrasting alternatives in the computational machines we have developed, and which have become almost indispensable tools in our everyday lives. I speak of computers, cell phones, game consoles, TVs, CDs, DVDs, e-books, and even automobiles, all of which depend on binary codes to process their information. What is a binary code? It is the alphabet of the computer chip. Unlike our twenty-six-letter alphabet, this alphabet has only two characters, 1 and 0. So the computer Alphabet Song would be very short and easy for preschoolers to learn. Those two characters are all that is needed in your phone to store the entire contents of the Library of Congress, as well as umpteen pictures of your grandchildren. These characters work like on-off switches, opposing states of information, a perfect example of the power of contrast, of opposition in nature. And if you will allow me a brief excursion into the realm of science fiction, let me ask this rather unsettling question: as our computer chips get smaller and smaller to the point that we are computing at the molecular level, will uncertainty lead to computers that have real choice—that have free will?

One of the starkest examples we face in our lives related to opposition in all things is the contrast between life and death. This aspect of existence doesn't apply to us only, or even just to things we would normally consider *living*. It extends even to the seemingly infinite and inanimate stars and galaxies that make up our universe. Did you know that stars have a life cycle just like people? We have learned through latter-day science that stars live out very interesting lives. They are born through the gravitational collapse of giant gas clouds in galaxies. As the gas collapses, it gets hotter and hotter as does any gas when it is compressed. When the mass of gas is star-sized, it gets hot enough for nuclear reactions to occur. These reactions produce lots of heat, which pushes outward on the star's material at the same time gravity is pulling the material in toward the center. This balance keeps the star roughly the same size for all of its adult life until the fuel for the nuclear reactions runs out. At that point, gravity can continue to make the star collapse, and as it does so it gets so dense that it can explode and die. Different kinds of stars face different ends, but this is the fate of large stars. And the debris from these explosions can then be used to form new stars and new planets. Of course, there are a lot more fascinating things that could be said on this subject, but the point is that stars, like people, face this ultimate dichotomy between life and death. Nothing seems to last forever, not even the unreachable stars. There is even discussion about the birth and death of the whole universe, with a big bang at the start and either a big crunch or a whimper at the end. You can consult your local cosmologist for details, but these concepts certainly echo the idea that the life of humans and gods embraces "one eternal round" (1 Nephi 10:19).

As we have seen repeatedly, Joseph Smith's vision of the world anticipated future science or at least was later shown to be compatible with science that was not known in his day. The scientific intellectuals of the early nineteenth century were convinced that the universe held no place for uncertainty but was a giant mechanism waiting to be unmasked so that everything in futurity could be calculated, at least in principle. Free will on the part of humankind was an elusion, so the idea of choice and accountability was unsupportable. It took a century to pass before modern science opened up the possibility of uncertainty at the atomic level, the very level at which intelligent thought has its source. And so once again, an apparent conflict between Joseph's theology and the science of his day was resolved with new discoveries in science after his time. I exercise my agency by choosing to see this as another testimony of Joseph's divine insights.

NOTE

1. Joseph Fielding Smith, *Teachings of the Prophet Joseph Smith*, Deseret Book, 1973, p. 353.

Chapter 12

Time—God, Angels, and Einstein

And thus there shall be the reckoning of the time of one planet above another, until thou come nigh unto Kolob, which Kolob is after the reckoning of the Lord's time; which Kolob is set nigh unto the throne of God, to govern all those planets which belong to the same order as that upon which thou standest. And it is given unto thee to know the set time of all the stars that are set to give light, until thou come near unto the throne of God. (Abraham 3:9–10)

One of the many things we take for granted in this modern world is the ease with which we can tell time. For example, in my house we have at least a dozen clocks, if you count the clocks on our oven and microwave oven. In addition, I wear a watch and I can consult my phone or my computer, so I don't have to look far to know what time it is any time of day. Furthermore, if I want to know what day it is, I can look at my wall calendar, phone, day planner, or computer—or I can ask a friend, who will no doubt wonder if I've lost track of all these items, and my mind as well. I need to know this information for important reasons. Is today the day I'm supposed to go to work or stay home? Is this my birthday, or more importantly, is it my wife's birthday or my anniversary? And if it is my anniversary, which anniversary is it? I need to know not only what year it is but also how many years have gone by between important events.

Things have not always been so simple. Go back more than a couple of hundred years, and in the western world it was uncommon to have a clock in your house or a pocket watch in your waistcoat. Only rich people were so lucky. If you wanted to know what time it was, you had to look at or listen to the clock on the city hall if you lived in the town; more likely if you lived in the countryside you looked at the sun and guessed, and if it was a cloudy day, you just guessed.

As to which day it was, you didn't have a wall calendar, but you might have an almanac. Mostly you relied on the church to guide you through the days of the year, with their special feast days (virtually every day celebrated some saint or event) and if you could remember to go to church every seventh day (or less), you would get updated on the calendar at that time. Church going had real practical value. And as you go back through the centuries, you find that whatever religion was dominant in your day and place, one of its principle contributions to your life was to make you aware of your place on the calendar. This was especially essential for peoples in former times, whose livelihoods were mostly agrarian, in that they needed to know if it was March or April and time to plant or not.

Ancient priests drew their knowledge of the calendar from the heavens, based on the regular clockwork-like motions of the sun, moon, planets, and stars. This dependence on the heavens has not changed—modern scientists and calendar makers likewise study the heavens to keep our calendars on track; it is a complicated business, but we are content to let them do this behind the scenes so we can get on with our daily lives.

We live out our lives against a background of time that seems so regular and normal to us that we assume that time flows the same way everywhere and from every perspective. But what if we lived on Venus? It takes Venus 224 earth days to circle the sun, but Venus rotates so slowly on its axis that a day on Venus lasts 117 earth days. Calendars and clocks on Venus would certainly look a lot different than here on earth—each *day* would last about half a *year*!

While traditionally there was a close alliance between religious institutions and the measurement of time, a relationship that lasted for thousands of years, by the time of Joseph Smith this cooperative arrangement seemed to be disintegrating—this not exclusively as it relates to the hourly clock of daily life, but also to the historical clock of the earth. Specifically, the science of geology was just coming into its own, and it was clear from that perspective that the earth was a lot older than clerics had been teaching. It was common among Christian denominations to take the King James version of the Bible quite literally when dealing with the chronology of creation found in Genesis. Thus, from pulpits everywhere came stern denunciations of newfangled ideas that the earth was more than a few thousand years old. Many still clung to chronologies like that proposed by Bishop Ussher of Ireland in the seventeenth century that creation could be dated exactly to October 22, 4004 BC, all carried out in exactly seven earth days. And indeed, many today equate faith in the Bible to this sort of literalism, faith not to the original text per se, but to the translation carried out by King James's scholars in the early 1600s.

Fortunately, modern revelation through Joseph Smith cast new light on this problem and largely closed the gap between what science teaches and what scripture intends. In his day and since, those attempting to harmonize the *old earth* teaching of science and the words of Genesis contended correctly that the original Hebrew could be translated either as a twenty-four-hour day or an indeterminate length of time. But the literalists would have none of it. So, while this battle raged between traditional Christian denominations and the scientific community, Joseph simply resolved the issue with his translation of Abraham's account of the Creation from the papyrus scrolls. Joseph had kept the word *day* in his retranslation of Genesis found in the Book of Moses (1830), but in the parallel account in Abraham (from 1835), he found the word *time* to be more appropriate than *day*. This interpretation was echoed in the temple endowment ceremony revealed in the 1840s. To Joseph, it was not the length of time that mattered so much as the orderly, step by step logical progression of the creative process. Each step in the process could take as long as was needed.

Did Joseph display any particular inclination toward settling the exact timing of creation? One clue into his thinking is found in a quote from the *Times and Seasons* newspaper, in which the Book of Abraham was first published in Nauvoo. Joseph's comment was reported by his friend and confidant William W. Phelps in 1844 not long before Joseph's death:

Well, now, Brother William, when the house of Israel begins to come into the glorious mysteries of the kingdom, and find that Jesus Christ, whose goings forth, as the prophets said, have been from of old, from eternity; and that eternity, agreeably to the records found in the catacombs of Egypt, has been going on in

105

this system, (not this world) almost two thousand five hundred and fifty five millions of years: and to know at the same time, that deists, geologists and others are trying to prove that matter must have existed hundreds of thousands of years;—it almost tempts the flesh to fly to God, or muster faith like Enoch to be translated and see and know as we are seen and known![1]

Clearly Joseph had no problem thinking of creation not in terms of thousands of years, but billions. His successor Brigham Young echoed this sentiment in 1871:

In these respects we differ from the [traditional] Christian world, for our religion will not clash with or contradict the facts of science in any particular. You may take geology, for instance, and it is a true science; not that I would say for a moment that all the conclusions and deductions of its professors are true, but its leading principles are; they are facts—they are eternal; and to assert that the Lord made this earth out of nothing is preposterous and impossible. God never made something out of nothing; it is not in the economy or law by which the worlds were, are, or will exist. There is an eternity before us, and it is full of matter; and if we but understand enough of the Lord and his ways, we would say that he took of this matter and organized this earth from it. How long it has been organized it is not for me to say, and I do not care anything about it. As for the Bible account of the creation we may say that the Lord gave it to Moses, or rather Moses obtained the history and traditions of the fathers, and from these picked out what he considered necessary, and that account has been handed down from age to age, and we have got it, no matter whether it is correct or not, and whether the Lord found the earth empty and void, whether he made it out of nothing or out of the rude elements; or whether he made it in six days or in as many millions of years, is and will remain a matter of speculation in the minds of men unless he give revelation on the subject. If we understood the process of creation there would be no mystery about it, it would be all reasonable and plain, for there is no mystery except to the ignorant.[2]

From these teachings we can conclude that while God has not clarified through his prophets the length of time it took to create the earth, current scientific thinking along these lines is not to be rejected out of hand based on what he has revealed so far. The jury is out on this question and it behooves us, like both Joseph and Brigham, to keep our minds open. And this counsel applies equally to saints and to scientists.

On a front that harmonizes well with science, Joseph Smith made it clear that the measurement of time is relative, saying in Doctrine and Covenants:

> In answer to the question—Is not the reckoning of God's time, angel's time, prophet's time, and man's time, according to the planet on which they reside? I answer, Yes. (D&C 130:4)

And this takes us back to our earlier discussion of what time would be like on Venus, or on any other planet in the universe. When the Lord speaks of days, or years, such measurements are relative to the stellar and planetary system involved. Thus, interpretations of references to time in scripture are open to discussion, and in the case of the creation story are much less important than the sequence and order presented. The Lord points to this relativism in reporting time in Doctrine and Covenants 88:

> And again, verily I say unto you, he hath given a law unto all things, by which they move in their times and their seasons; And their courses are fixed, even the courses of the heavens and the earth, which comprehend the earth and all the planets. And they give light to each other in their times and in their seasons, in their minutes, in their hours, in their days, in their weeks, in their months, in their years—all these are one year with God, but not with man. The earth rolls upon her wings, and the sun giveth his light by day, and the moon giveth her light by night, and the stars also give their light, as they roll upon their wings in their glory, in the midst of the power of God. (D&C 88:42–45)

This is one important point to keep in mind when trying to understand how time relates to God and his works: the measurement of time is relative to the observer and his home in the universe.

But there is another interesting aspect of time that we learned about long after Joseph's death and that opens up new insights into the nature of time itself. This newly discovered aspect of time influences how time appears to different observers in our universe. It is not as simple as the differences between planetary orbits or the rates of planetary revolution. Instead, it deals with differences in the way time appears *to progress* from one observer to the next.

We are so used to time progressing in the same way and at the same rate throughout our lives that we are left with the impression that it must be the same throughout the universe. We think of time as a constant backdrop against which all events play out. But Einstein, the myth buster of common sense, has revealed that this is not so. Some of his most dramatic and unsettling revelations (and I think that these are indeed revelations as we understand them, given that God is the source of all enlightenment) deal with the passage of time itself. Just as he showed that space is not a constant but can be warped to produce the effects of gravity, so he showed that time is also flexible. Indeed, his model couples time and space together, so that physicists no longer speak of space and time but of *space-time*.

Whole textbooks are written to explain the origins and meaning of Einstein's model of space-time, and it is not my purpose here to prepare you for a PhD in physics. Rather, let me simply summarize some of Einstein's findings. The term that is most commonly applied to Einstein's theories is *relativity*, and that has to do with the fact that the rate at which time passes is *relative* to the observer who is measuring it. Let's look at a few scenarios.

- Let's say you are on the earth and observing the clock on a spaceship moving away from you. If the ship is moving at a few thousand miles per hour, like the fastest space probe we've launched to date, the clock on the ship will appear to be advancing at almost exactly the same rate as your watch here on earth. But if the spaceship is moving at a constant speed at close to the speed of light (186,000 miles per second), to you here on earth the clock on the spaceship will seem to be running much more slowly than your watch. And indeed, if the ship were to achieve the speed of light itself, the observer on earth would see that the clock on the ship had stopped altogether. Now, it turns out that another of Einstein's rules is that the ship cannot reach exactly the speed of light (for reasons we won't go into), but in theory it can get very close.

- Now here's something even more bizarre: The astronaut on the spaceship sees the mirror image of what we just described. To him, it appears that the earth is moving away from him (backwards) at close to the speed of light. In other words, he can think of the situation from his own point of view—he is standing still and it is the earth that is moving (hence the term relativity—what is happening can always be described relative to the point of view, sometimes called the *frame of reference*, of the observer). Now, he sees the clock in his spaceship advancing at the normal rate, whereas when he looks at your watch on earth, it is your watch that appears to be running slow. So, each observer sees his clock running normally, while the other's is running slow. The rate of passage of time is relative!

- But that's not the only situation in which time seems to slow down. Einstein's theories also show that when a clock finds itself in a strong gravitational field, perhaps near a heavy star, to an external observer far away, time on that distant clock slows down. This effect is small except near very heavy objects like neutron stars or black holes. But near a black hole, especially the super massive ones at the centers of galaxies, this effect can be very large. For example, if we were to watch a spaceship fall into a black hole, it would come to the point where the clock on the ship seemed to almost stop, and with it the forward movement of the ship itself. To the observer far away, it would appear that time has stopped (or nearly so) near the black hole. This bizarre behavior can make for some great science fiction!

- These effects don't just apply to mechanical or electronic clocks. Time itself is slowing down, so the rate at which everything is happening on the ship is affected, including the rate at which people seem to move and even to age. To an external observer looking at a spaceship moving close to the speed of light, the astronaut on the ship would seem to be frozen in mid-stride; he would not age but would seem to live almost forever in this frozen attitude. By the same token, to an external observer looking at a spaceship near a black hole, the astronaut in the ship would appear to move and age more slowly. So if one of two twins were the astronaut and his twin brother was the external distant observer, when the astronaut returned to earth, he would indeed be physically much younger than his twin—theoretically one twin could be celebrating his thirtieth birthday on the same day the other is celebrating his eightieth birthday, even though they were originally born on earth on the same day! If you want to live a long life (at least from the point of view of your friends), park yourself near a black hole for a while.

You might be rolling your eyes at this point and thinking that scientists must have lost their collective minds to believe anything so outlandish as what I've just described. And it's true that these were hard ideas to swallow even by the scientific community when first presented. But think back to our chapter on faith in science. Scientists now have a great deal of faith in Einstein's model because in repeated experiments we see that the model is borne out. We can't send spaceships at close to the speed of light, but we can accelerate small particles to close to the speed of light in giant particle accelerators. These small particles can decay (break apart) into even smaller particles at very predictable rates in time. We observe that when these particles are accelerated to close to the speed of light, they decay more slowly, to the exact degree that Einstein predicts. Furthermore, although we can't look at clocks close to black holes, we have measured the difference in the rate of highly accurate electronic clocks when close to the earth compared to the rate of the same clocks when further away from the earth's gravitational field. We find that there is a tiny difference in the measured rate of time passing when close to the earth versus further away. The measured effect of the earth's gravitation on the rate of passage of time is exactly what Einstein predicted. In fact, the calculations needed to make your GPS system work require that these effects be accounted for, given that the satellites used in GPS have clocks that run a little faster than clocks on earth, like the clock in your cell phone. If these *relativistic* effects weren't included in the calculations, your GPS would have you driving off cliffs and into the ocean within a few hours. These and countless other experimental results confirm Einstein's view to the point that faith in his model is now firm.

This leads us to the second important point to keep in mind when trying to understand how time relates to God and his works: the rate of passage of time for any observer depends not only on the motion of his planet, but on his speed relative to us and the gravitational field around him versus that around us. Time itself is flexible! And the measurement of time for God, angels, and men can differ substantially if these factors come into play.

It is clear from what he has revealed that despite our close relationship to God, the current state in which we find ourselves must be very different from his immortal and exalted state. So, it is very likely that he perceives time in a very different way than do we. Indeed, Joseph is reported to have said:

> The great Jehovah contemplated the whole of the events connected with the earth, pertaining to the plan of salvation, before it rolled into existence, or ever "the morning stars sang together" for joy; the past, the present, and the future were and are, with Him, one eternal "now."[3]

We certainly can't claim to understand fully God's relationship to time. For instance, opinions differ about how God perceives the future, and what does it mean that the past, present, and future are for him "one eternal now"? If the God we know exists in real space, does he not also exist in real time? In the semi-official publication *The Encyclopedia of Mormonism* we find this question addressed in a rather academic style:

> The thesis that God is beyond time has sometimes been introduced to account for God's omniscience or foreknowledge. Only if God is somehow transtemporal [existing outside of time], it is argued, can he view past, present, and future as "one eternal now." This position is assumed by much postbiblical theology. But, again, this leads to contradiction: What will happen in the infinite future is now happening to God. But "now" and "happening" are temporal words that imply both duration and change. For Latter-day Saints, as for the Bible, God's omniscience is "in time." God anticipates the future. It is "present" before him, but it is still future. When the future occurs, it will occur for the first time to him as to his creatures. The traditional concept of "out-of-time" omniscience does not derive either from the Old or the New Testament but is borrowed from Greek philosophy.[4]

The Doctrine and Covenants throws further light on the question of God's relationship to time:

> The seventh angel shall sound his trump; and he shall stand forth upon the land and upon the sea, and swear in the name of him who sitteth upon the throne, that there shall be time no longer; and Satan shall be bound, that old serpent, who is called the devil, and shall not be loosed for the space of a thousand years. (D&C 88:110)

Clearly, such statements as "there shall be time no longer" must mean that the *effects* of time are erased, not time itself, else how could thereafter be a period of a thousand years and events to follow?

On a more individual level, one factor that may influence one's perception of the rate at which time passes may be historical perspective. As a simple example, you may have noticed, as have I, that as we age, time seems to pass more quickly, even though our reason tells us that the clock is ticking at the same rate as before, and at the same rate as for those young whipper-snappers around us. I can remember as a child that it seemed to take forever for the clock in my grade school classroom to grind its way through the last hour of the school day; whereas today the last hour of even the most boring presentation seems to zoom by. To a child, an hour represents a much larger percentage of his or her lifespan than to a seventy-year old. Imagine what a small percentage of the Lord's perceived lifetime (virtually infinite!) that an hour or a day or even a year would represent. Perhaps the years or even the eons would seem to zoom by to one having such a godly perspective of time.

Whatever the answer to these interesting theological questions, it is clear that both science and Joseph Smith's theology speak of time as relative in certain senses, and on this point both sides can certainly agree. In Joseph's day, much was understood about the difference in time between planets as related to their orbits and rates of rotation. But the more advanced concepts related to geologic time and Einstein's ideas were yet to be discovered. The relatively few references to time in Joseph's sermons and revealed scriptures are certainly forward looking and compatible with twenty-first century scientific theories about time and space.

It would be tempting at this point to speculate about the relationship between modern theories of time dilation à la Einstein and the time experienced in the heavens by angels, translated beings, and gods. But though these ideas open up wonderful opportunities for science fiction and for family discussions on late-night campouts, that has not been the objective of our discussion here. Rather, I have attempted to point out that time is much more complex than we would be inclined to imagine, and that when considering references to time in scripture, we should keep this in mind. When the Lord speaks of days, years, or futurity his vastly superior understanding of and perspective of time may be an attempt to convey much more than our simple ideas might lead us to assume. We may discover that even with Einstein's insights, we have only scratched the surface in our understanding of time. Along with spirit, physical matter, and space, time may be one of the elements that he is able to manipulate in bringing about his glorious purposes for his own benefit and ultimately ours as well. It is striking that these modern scientific concepts of relative time, unknown in Joseph Smith's day, are very much consistent with his limited teachings and revelations on this subject.

NOTES

1. *Times and Seasons*, Nauvoo, Illinois, December 31, 1844, **5**, p. 758; available as a free e-book on Google Books, found on p. 375 of that e-book.
2. *Journal of Discourses*, Albert Carrington Pub., Liverpool, 1872, **14**, p. 116; Brigham Young discourse, May 14, 1871.
3. Joseph Fielding Smith, *Teachings of the Prophet Joseph Smith*, Deseret Book, 1973, p. 220.
4. Kent E. Robson, "Time and Eternity," *Encyclopedia of Mormonism*, Daniel H. Ludlow, ed., Macmillan Publishing Company, 1st edition, 1992; available free online at eom.byu.edu and searchable by topic.

Chapter 13

THE DOGMA TRAP

*To become a joint heir of the heirship of the Son, one must put away all his false traditions. (*Teachings of the Prophet Joseph Smith, p. 321)

In the middle of the thirteenth century, a Dominican friar named Thomas Aquinas was instrumental in laying the foundation of accepted cosmology for centuries to come, as mentioned in previous chapters. His teachings about cosmology took on the aura of dogma, and so present us with a handy case study of dogmatic belief. To start, let's clarify the meaning of *cosmology*. Cosmology is a relatively modern term and is the branch of natural philosophy that describes the structure and origins of the universe. Although he would not have used this term, Aquinas was definitely interested in the origins and structure of the world, particularly as related to Christian scripture and doctrine.

Aquinas had been born in a small town in the center of the Italian peninsula—you'll remember that Italy as a country didn't exist in those days. As a member of the gentry, he was educated from an early age, and despite his family's going to the extreme of imprisoning him for a year to prevent him from doing so, he entered the Dominican monastic order. Thereafter, he was tutored under the finest mentors of the age in Paris and elsewhere, moved to and taught at several respected schools, published widely, and, in short, followed the same kind of career path that leads to fame and fortune in our modern academic world. His lasting legacy resides in his writings, chief among them the grand work entitled *Summa Theologica.* Several of his writings became so widely used in the schools of the so-called *Scholastics* that for centuries, even until now, they became a standard part of the theological curriculum. And as is often true today, so it was then, "He who writes the textbook governs the curriculum." Indeed, Aquinas's ideas became so well entrenched that they took on the special status we call dogma.

What is dogma? Dogma is unquestionable belief—belief so strong that no amount of evidence or rational argument to the contrary can budge it. No discussion allowed! For our purposes here, let's define two different levels of dogma. Specifically, we'll make a distinction between dogma as I would spell it with a capital letter *D* and that beginning with the lowercase *d*.

First, capital letter Dogma. Every belief system, religious or otherwise, has a certain set of fundamental axioms or assumptions upon which all other beliefs are based, and without which the belief system would collapse. Religious systems, such as Christianity or Islam often designate formal *Dogmata*, referring to very specific points of belief, well formulated and often published, which true practitioners of the faith must adhere to. For instance, Christians couldn't really be believing Christians if they didn't believe that Christ existed. Science also has its own fundamental beliefs, as we described in the earlier chapter "Faith in Religion and Science."

In this current chapter, we will focus primarily on the kind of dogma spelled with a lowercase *d*, dogma in the broader and more general sense—including ideas that are widely held as dogma even though they are not fundamental to the belief system and may not have been given any formal ratification. Within the belief system, one person may hold a particular belief dogmatically, while another may not. So we are talking about individual beliefs that are not foundational to the belief system, but which have become unquestionable in the minds of at least some people, perhaps most. One can be dogmatic about almost anything, formalized or otherwise, religious or scientific, and because this can be an impediment to finding truth, it involves a trap we should be aware of and avoid where possible.

Now back to our story. Aquinas was well respected in his day, and his writings have endured the test of time because he was indeed a giant intellect. He was given the moniker Doctor Angelicus (which means exactly what it sounds like) and made a saint not long after his death. He is given much credit for his efforts to harmonize revealed religious truth with the best science and philosophy of his day. Like many today, he took the position that faith and reason are both legitimate sources of truth and that they can and must mutually conform to the *same* truth. He made the argument that the study of nature and the application of reason were equally valid with revelation in discerning the nature of God and his creations.

The best science of Aquinas's day was that of the ancient Greek philosophers, like Alexander the Great's tutor Aristotle, whose writings were in the process of being rediscovered, or better said, returned to the western world through the medium of the Islamic world. Fifteen centuries earlier, Aristotle had laid out a model of the universe, based on observation and reason, which had endured, with some modifications, for all that time. As a reminder, the basic elements of the simplest form of Aristotle's model were these: We have the corrupt earth at the center (or bottom) of the universe, the planets, or *wanderers* (including the sun and moon), orbiting around it in circles generated by the motion of perfect crystalline spheres composed of the heavenly quintessence, and the fixed stars beyond embedded in another perfect crystalline sphere.

This all seemed quite consistent with scripture to Aquinas; so, in keeping with his effort to bring together the truths of religion and natural philosophy (science) as understood in his day, Aquinas pictured the Christian cosmos in harmony with Aristotle's model. We find the earth at the center (bottom or lowest point) as the proper place for the home of man, the central focus of God's creation. Above we see the perfect, unchangeable heavens in concentric spheres, homes to the planets. But instead of Greek gods associated with these spheres, in keeping with his theology, these spheres became the homes to various ranks of angels. Beyond the outermost sphere was the inscrutable realm of God, creator and unmoved mover of all. And in the depths under the earth, at the center of the world where all corrupt things had fallen, was the realm of Satan and hell.

The harmonizing of science and religion in this way was a great strengthener of faith for Christians. The idea that the best that science had to offer was consistent with orthodox teaching held tremendous appeal, and so this cosmological model was taught authoritatively for hundreds of years in the universities almost without question. Who would dare question such beautiful ideas?

Of course, you recognize that this is not how we picture the universe today. The switch among academics to a sun-centered solar system and ultimately to galaxies and an almost infinite universe with billions of trillions of observable stars and solar systems was not easy. How so? Well, imagine yourself a university don in the sixteenth or seventeenth centuries, hundreds of years after Aquinas, standing in front of a class of enthralled disciples, in the majesty of your academic gown, reciting in high-sounding tones the time-honored and venerated truth of the Aristotelian model of the world. Generations upon generations of your predecessor professors have done likewise and won admiration and esteem. Why should you doubt the absolute truth of it? And what would you do, then, if an upstart like Copernicus or Galileo came along in the sixteenth and seventeenth centuries with new observations and a new sun-centered model that refuted your teachings? In your mind, the Aristotelian model (or shall we call it the Scholastic model) of the cosmos has become more than a good idea—it has become entrenched to the point of being unquestionable—in other words, to you it has become *dogma* (note the lowercase *d*). Would it not be unsettling to you that these men were promoting a new sun-centered model with heavenly bodies that are not perfect homes for angels? Why take them seriously if dogma dictates otherwise? Besides, to accept their new science would be tantamount to coming down from your ivory tower and admitting you were wrong—and there goes your reputation, and maybe your retirement pension.

Now to be fair, not all academics and churchmen (who for the most part *were* the academics at that time) felt this way. After all, these ideas were not necessary and fundamental to Christianity; they had simply become dogma in the minds of many due to their longevity. By contrast, some scholars were open to new ideas. Yet enough were not, many of them in powerful positions, so that to quote from Stephen Mason's book, *A History of the Sciences*:

> In 1615 Galileo was summoned before the Inquisition at Rome, and there he was made to abjure the Copernican theory [on pain of death]. The propositions that the earth rotated on its axis and that it moved round the sun, were officially declared to be false and heretical, and in 1616 the work of Copernicus was placed on the Index of prohibited books, not to be removed until 1835.[1]

In the end, Galileo spent the latter decade of his life under house imprisonment by the Vatican over this new cosmology and was lucky to escape with his life, a victim of dogmatic thinking. To be fair to the Roman Catholic Church, many Protestants were no less dogmatic about the issue, and both Luther and Calvin, who were contemporaries of Copernicus, rejected this new science as heretical as well.

As to the final outcome of our story, in the end, scientists (sooner) and religionists (later), both came to accept the transition to a new model of the universe. Today, virtually every human on the planet demonstrates not a single qualm in accepting a universe consistent with the sun-centered solar system within an unimaginably large number of stars and galaxies. Yet we shouldn't take for granted that this has always been so. For many who adhered dogmatically to their traditions, it was a long, agonizing slog to make the transition. And taking the dogmatic approach on a question that was not fundamental to their religious faith (not Dogma as we have defined it) was the primary slogifying influence, if you'll permit me to invent that new unscientific term.

The story we've reviewed illustrates as well as any how the confluence of science and religion provides a perfect opportunity for exposing dogmatic views. We mustn't assume, however, that it was only religious practitioners who fell into the dogma trap on this occasion. Many scientists were slow to give up their traditional teachings as well; moreover, it would be hard to make much of a distinction between these two groups (scientists and religionists) in that day, as the academy was much different then than it is now in the sense that the two groups were composed largely of the same persons. The university and the research laboratory in those days were most often staffed by professor priests or monks, and indeed, Copernicus himself belonged to a minor monastic order and received his doctorate in canon (church) law, not in natural philosophy. Even those not formally associated with the priesthood made religious thinking an integral part of their academic work. This state of affairs persisted for centuries until not that long ago. Even Newton, who became known as the father of the mechanical universe in the eighteenth century, found himself working at least as much on Bible-related enquiries as on the physical world that won him his reputation. Indeed, Newton had to be careful to obfuscate his true religious beliefs, many of which were not orthodox, in order to maintain his Lucasian Chair at Cambridge University.

Science and religion share at least one common goal that might be summarized as follows: to help us understand the world we live in—how to cope with it, how to control it, how to view our proper place in it, and how to achieve the greatest possible personal fulfillment from it. Given that the pursuit of truth is central to the mission statements (to use a modern term) of both these endeavors, dogmatic thinking can present a real problem, as the above story amply illustrates. To elaborate, let's consider three theses:

1. Both religion and science are grounded in faith.
2. Belief systems in both arenas embrace principles ranging across a spectrum of significance.
3. Beliefs in both arenas are susceptible to dogma traps which impede the pursuit of truth.

Thesis 1: We have already discussed in a previous chapter how both science and religion are grounded in faith. In the realm of religion, reference to faith goes almost without saying. But of course, the principle applies equally to science. First of all, scientists have faith in the inherent order in the natural world and the human ability to reveal that order. Closer to home, you have undoubtedly taken at least one science class in your life (perhaps welcome, perhaps not). And as you studied the structure of the atom or the Krebs cycle in living systems, did you not take it on faith that the instructor wasn't just making it all up, and that the $200 you spent on that textbook wasn't an entire waste because the content of every beautifully illustrated page wasn't just one gigantic fraud? Yes, of course you did—you took that on faith, so you didn't drop the class.

The only way science can advance is if each successive generation of scientists has faith in the claims of careful observation, analysis, and reporting of its predecessors. None of us has time to go back and double check the painstaking work of Rutherford or Pauling or Watson and Crick. Newton is said to have claimed that he saw further because he was standing on the shoulders of giants, but he had to have faith that those giants weren't really just a bunch of leprechauns standing on each others' shoulders in an oversized lab coat. So it is with all of scientific advances.

Thesis 2: Let's consider how belief systems in both science and religion embrace principles ranging across a spectrum of significance. By significance I mean the relative importance of a principle or belief to the overall integrity of the belief system. This spectrum ranges from belief in principles that are foundational to the system at one extreme to those which are trivial at the other extreme. For example, on the foundational end of the spectrum, many religions post formal articles of faith. The restored Church of Jesus Christ of Latter-day Saints has thirteen; the National Baptist Convention has eighteen; Maimonides listed Thirteen Fundamental Principles for the Jewish faith; Islam lists six. And of course, the big daddy of articles of faith for most Christians is the Nicene Creed in its various flavors. For religious believers, these points are not negotiable. The belief system would collapse without them. They are on the *extremely significant* end of the significance spectrum. So, it is not surprising that adherents to each religion would treat them as Dogma. For Latter-day Saints, an example on the other end of the spectrum might be a belief that Kolob is located on the star Sirius or at the supermassive black hole at the center of the Milky Way. It is not likely to cause anyone to lose their faith in the restored Church if such speculative beliefs turn out to be unfounded.

Science also has its articles of faith, as listed in the previous chapter dealing with faith. You will recall that these include the reality of existence, causality, and the universality of natural law in both space and time. It is interesting that these very basic and essential components of the scientific endeavor are seldom discussed or even given a thought by practicing scientists except when teaching introductory general science classes. Like articles of faith in religion, they are so grounded in our psyche that they go not only without saying, but without thinking. They are treated as Dogma as one would expect. On the other end of the significance spectrum would be a belief that dark matter is composed of neutrinos (a known subatomic particle of almost no mass and no charge). One would not entirely abandon belief in the scientific process if this idea turned out to be wrong.

Clearly, in both science and religion there are many beliefs which are not fundamental to the belief system. In fact, most beliefs would fall into this category. For example, Lord Kelvin (the nineteenth century don of science) and my college chemistry textbook and many experts over the years have testified to me that the second law of thermodynamics is true, that no one has ever observed otherwise—so I believe them and move on. But this law is not foundational to science—science would not completely fall apart if this principle were replaced with something better. So, even though I believe in this law fervently, the question for me is this: can I be justified in being dogmatic about this principle? Or better said: would I be wise to be dogmatic about it? Should I defend it to the death even if faced with rational arguments or evidence to the contrary? The answer is no. This law is not absolutely fundamental to the scientific enterprise. While I have a strong faith in this principle, being dogmatic about it would be going too far. I'd be wise to keep my eyes open and be ready for that Nobel prize if I happen to notice a provable system that does not obey the second law. By taking this position, I avoid falling into a trap, a dogma trap, that would prevent me from advancing my understanding. The wise approach for the true seeker of truth is to keep the mind open at least a crack.

Although this chapter rather puts dogma in a negative light, let me clarify that just because a belief is held to be dogma does not mean that it is intrinsically false or bad. If dogmatism is a problem, as it often is, the problem is not with the belief itself but with the holder of the belief. This is an important distinction. Let's take an example from science: the idea of reproducibility. That's the idea that scientists should believe in an observation and its explanation only if it can be made to happen or be observed over and over again with the same result. Some scientists have put this idea right at the extreme end of importance along the significance spectrum and consider it as dogma—any claim must meet this test to be considered true. But like any good principle, the requirement for reproducibility can be carried too far. The problem arises when some scientists dogmatically insist that it be used to test the validity of all hypotheses, scientific or otherwise—it becomes an *unquestionable* principle applicable to all situations in their minds. No one is allowed to question or modify it under any circumstance. Period, end of discussion. It's my way or the highway. It's Galileo in prison. It's the heretic in the fire. It's not just an article of faith, it's the one and only true way. If any claims, especially religious claims, can't pass this test, they are bogus.

Yet not all scientists share this attitude about the principle of reproducibility. Where on the significance spectrum an idea like reproducibility finds itself is often a matter of individual choice. Many scientists would put reproducibility a bit closer to the middle of the significance spectrum. Certainly, all would agree that for a *scientific* assertion to be established as true, it must be underpinned by observations that are reproducible. It just goes without saying. I believe in the need for reproducibility, my colleagues in chemistry believe in it; we all apply it almost religiously in our practice of science. It is a good principle in scientific research. But if the argument is made that for *any* belief to be valid it must pass the test of reproducibility, then a good working principle has taken on the unwarranted aspect of dogma and becomes not a useful tool in the pursuit of truth, but an impediment. For example, reproducibility, or rather the lack of it, has been used as an argument against claims in religion. In science, reproducibility of observations serves as the basis for faith; in religion, faith-promoting events are rare and not predictable and therefore not reproducible in the scientific sense; but that doesn't mean they aren't real. Let me ask you: is an event that happens only once every few hundred or thousand years to one person but not another not real because it is rare?

Along these lines, the high priest of atheism may bear his testimony that there is no God because you cannot observe him scientifically. He may say: how can you believe in God—have you seen him? The religionist might answer: how can you believe in electrons—have you seen one? In response, the atheist may answer—no, but I have seen their effects reproducibly in the laboratory. And the religionist may answer—in the same way, I have seen the effects of God in my life and the lives of others. I can't measure the latter kind of effect quantitatively or make it happen at will as in a laboratory, but it is real to me. In both cases, the proponents observe the effects (the one of God, the other of the electron), deduces the existence, and have faith that their conclusion is correct. Furthermore, in both cases the proponent often relies with faith on the testimony of witnesses—those who have more direct experience. The religionist strengthens his faith in the testimony of prophets who have seen or had close experiences of the divine; the scientist has faith in the testimony of predecessor scientists who have performed and reported the results of their experiments. Many scientists believe that there is more to truth than what science has been able to reveal with our senses and our machines, and therefore they keep an open mind to the possibility that religion may have something to add. They understand that when applied dogmatically, the idea that "seeing is believing" (and *only* seeing reproducibly) is a trap that can prevent one from achieving a fulness of truth.

In summary, we have seen examples of bedrock articles of faith (Dogma) in both science and religion, as well as examples of what we might call lesser articles of faith which may or may not be held as dogma depending on the person. Once people have embraced a certain bedrock set of beliefs, such as science or Latter-day Saint theology, they are free within those parameters to seek out and construct other beliefs of lesser surety within the confines of that belief system. It is among the latter beliefs where progress against dogmatic thinking can yield the most likely rewards. The danger arises when a person develops a belief which at first is accepted as plausible, but which over time has been repeated so often, challenged so seldom, become so comfortable, that it gradually and inexorably approaches the status of unquestionable. Without hardly realizing it, a person can become dogmatic about a particular idea, even though it is not a necessary component of their belief system. This is where we often run into trouble, and this leads me to the third thesis.

Thesis 3: Belief systems in both arenas are susceptible to dogma traps which impede the pursuit of truth.

Perhaps the best approach to clarifying this point is with a series of examples. We've seen already how the dogmatic adherence to the Aristotelian model of the cosmos impeded the advancement of our understanding of astronomy and cosmology, impacting both the scientific and the religious camps. I'll take my next example from the arena of scientific research with an episode much closer to home and to our own day.

In March 1989, two scientists at the University of Utah, Stan Pons and Martin Fleischmann, announced that they had discovered cold fusion. The story is a fascinating one, and lengthy books have been written about this episode—it even impacted BYU and me personally, as I was serving as Brigham Young University's Director of Research at the time. Just to put their discovery in perspective for those unfamiliar with nuclear science, nuclear fusion is the process that powers the sun. It comes about when the positively charged nuclei of two atoms smash together and combine (*fuse*) to form a single heavier nucleus plus some byproducts, including a lot of energy. In order to fuse, the nuclei have to get extremely close to one another. Scientists have been trying to create sustained fusion reactions on earth for decades, but the problem is that the positively charged nuclei of the atoms repel one another so effectively that it's almost impossible to get them close enough to fuse.

The first significant success in creating fusion on earth was to generate uncontrolled fusion in the form of a hydrogen bomb (H bomb). This isn't the kind of atomic *fission* bomb dropped on Hiroshima or Nagasaki—it's much more powerful than that. In fact, it takes the heat of an atomic fission bomb to raise the temperature of the hydrogen atoms high enough so that the atoms are moving fast enough to overcome their mutual repulsion and fuse. But H bombs aren't a good way to generate electricity—they tend to destroy stuff—so the holy grail of fusion research has been to find a way to make fusion occur under controlled conditions. Normally, initiating fusion would require raising the temperature of the hydrogen to millions of degrees, as on the sun, but here's the rub: what kind of container could house this reaction without being vaporized at the millions of degrees required? Ingenious but very expensive ways of containing this reaction have been investigated. Indeed, I can remember as a boy being promised that within a few decades, controlled fusion would be operational, and limitless energy would be available to power human civilization for millions of years into the future. By now, decades have come and gone and we're still not much closer to making controlled fusion a reality, leading to the oft quoted cynical saying, "Fusion is the energy source of the future and always will be."

Given this state of affairs, the announcement of Pons and Fleishman that they had achieved fusion at room temperature came as a real bombshell to the scientific community. If true, it would sidestep the high temperature requirements altogether and make the scientists and the university very Very VERY rich. But there was a problem: the only evidence these researchers had for fusion in their case was a great deal of heat from their tabletop reactor—so much so, they said, that it melted its way down through the tabletop. From the beginning, there were serious problems with this claim:

- First, heat is not a sure signature of a nuclear process like nuclear fusion; simpler explanations would involve chemical processes which had nothing to do with nuclear interactions.
- Second, their results were not reproducible even in their own laboratory.
- Third, as time went by and other scientists tried, the result could not be reproduced in laboratories around the world.
- Fourth, no one in the Pons/Fleishman lab or in other labs could find any of the telltale signs (biproducts) of a nuclear process, such as neutrons or gamma rays.
- Fifth, their claim flew in the face of a huge body of accepted knowledge about nuclear processes. If their claim were true, not only would it solve the energy needs of the world, the whole

science of nuclear processes, developed over the previous eighty years, would have to be rewritten.

- Sixth, Pons and Fleishman should have been dead, killed by the high-energy particle biproducts of the nuclear reaction. They weren't.

How does this episode relate to our topic here? It has to do with the gradual creep in the minds of these scientists toward thinking of their claims dogmatically. First, let's admit that anyone, including a scientist, can make an honest mistake. That's not the point. The point is that as time went by and as more and more evidence mounted that what they observed was not fusion, instead of admitting their mistake, the scientists became more and more defensive and insistent that they were dealing with fusion processes. If their result did not square with current nuclear theory, then the entire body of nuclear physics developed by thousands of scientists over the last century needed to be completely revised. It is clear that over time, their belief was sliding gradually toward the dogma extreme—their faith in their belief could not be shaken by any amount of evidence to the contrary. Pons and Fleishman had fallen into the dogma trap. And they weren't the only ones. There are true believers in cold fusion among a tiny minority of scientists to this very day, along with people willing to back them with funding.

In another example, this time in the realm of religion, Joseph Smith often became frustrated with the people of his day, both within and without the Church, in trying to introduce to them his ever-widening vision of eternal principles. Toward the end of his life, he is quoted as saying:

> There has been a great difficulty in getting anything into the heads of this generation. It has been like splitting hemlock knots with a corn-dodger [a piece of corn bread] for a wedge and a pumpkin for a beetle [a mallet]. . . . I have tried for a number of years to get the minds of the Saints prepared to receive the things of God; but we frequently see some of them, after suffering all they have for the work of God, will fly to pieces like glass as soon as anything comes that is contrary to their traditions.[2]

The traditions that Joseph bemoans are essentially beliefs that the Saints have come to regard as dogma—and finding themselves in the dogma trap, their progress toward ultimate truth and exaltation was hindered.

Doctrine and Covenants 19 provides us an example of just how easily we can fall into a trap believing dogmatically that we understand a principle when in fact we don't. Speaking of the judgment of the wicked, the Lord states:

> It is not written that there shall be no end to this torment, but it is written *endless torment*. Again, it is written *eternal damnation*. . . . Wherefore, I will explain unto you this mystery. . . . For, behold, I am endless, and the punishment which is given from my hand is endless punishment, for Endless is my name. Wherefore—Eternal punishment is God's punishment. Endless punishment is God's punishment. (D&C 19:6–7, 8, 10–12)

Now before this clarification, I'm sure there was absolutely no doubt in almost anyone's mind what "endless punishment" meant—it was a seemingly obvious point of dogma, albeit a rather minor one, a lesser article of faith if you will. There probably wasn't a Christian minister alive who wouldn't argue most vehemently that God intended to inflict punishment on the wicked for all eternity to come. Yet here is an example of the genius of Joseph Smith—he was not dogmatic about his beliefs; and that meant he was teachable and open to the truth as God revealed it. And frankly, to me this truth makes a lot more sense than inflicting infinite punishment on a person for a finite number of sins.

Finally, here's another brief example of the dogma trap catching some scientists in its clutches. In the early twentieth century a meteorologist from Germany named Alfred Wegener followed up on an observation that most children, including me and probably you, have made about the map of the continents—namely that the eastern outline of the American continents roughly matches that of western Europe and Africa. Various other similarities including fossil species and land formations also seemed to line up on both sides of the Atlantic, leaving the scientific community puzzled as to the cause. So, Wegener proposed that at some time in the distant past, the continents must have been joined and then broke apart and drifted in opposite directions to form the Atlantic Ocean. For his trouble, he was viciously attacked by the geological scientific establishment, partly on the grounds that there was no known mechanism for continents to move, and therefore it was dogmatically believed that this was impossible. Furthermore, Wegener had the temerity to not be a geologist.

It was not until after Wegener's untimely death by freezing in Greenland (an ironic way to go for a meteorologist) that plate tectonics became one of the rock-solid (if I may apply the pun) principles of terrestrial geology. Plate tectonics describes the surface of the earth as consisting of a number of rocky plates which float on a liquid-like layer below. According to this model the Atlantic ocean was formed when a large plate that included all of North and South America, Africa, and Eurasia split apart into two pieces millions of years ago. The Americas drifted westward; Eurasia and Africa drifted eastward and water filled the gap in between forming the Atlantic. This model is now widely accepted, but not without having endured the strain of overcoming dogmatic opposition to Wegener's proposal and to the man himself.

A similar dogmatic adherence, this time to uniformitarianism, was the cause for foot-dragging among geologists before accepting the catastrophe-oriented explanation for the demise of the dinosaurs sixty-five million years ago by asteroid impact. Uniformitarianism even sounds like a religion, doesn't it? On the contrary, it is the early belief among geologists that all processes in geology are slow and steady, making gradual changes over millions of years. This belief gradually strengthened into virtual dogma by the middle of the twentieth century, so that when strong evidence was found that the dinosaurs were wiped out by the impact of an asteroid, the idea was opposed vehemently by the scientific establishment. Such an impact did not fit into the dogma that all processes in geology had to occur slowly over time—so the asteroid hypothesis was derided as simplistic or impossible. Yet, just as three hundred years ago the strength of evidence ultimately overcame the Aristotelian dogma about the structure of the universe, so the strength of recent evidence has overcome the dogma of uniformitarianism; and now the idea that the dinosaurs were done in by asteroid is widely accepted. It turns out that uniformitarianism isn't wrong; it's just not the *only* answer as dogmatists had insisted.

The dinosaur example reemphasizes that an idea that is held dogmatically is not by definition false, but rather that the fault lies with the believer. Geologists still hold to the idea of uniformitarianism—that is, to the idea that most geological processes are indeed slow and occur over long periods of time. But this true concept is now modified to include the possibility of occasional catastrophes that induce sudden changes as well. The problem with this episode in the history of science is that some scientists had closed their minds to any modification of their closely held beliefs and therefore threw up impediments to innovation based not on evidence but on what we might call prejudice. And this is the danger of the dogma trap.

There are lots of examples we could cite here from both science and religion where even well-educated men and women have fallen into the dogma trap. We spoke earlier in this chapter about scientists who insist that because the claims of religion cannot meet the test of scientific reproducibility, they are not valid, and how this assertion for some has taken on the aura of dogma. The author Lewis Vaughn in his book *The Power of Critical Thinking* defines a term for this almost religious mode of thought: *Scientism*. He states:

> Science is not scientism. One definition of scientism is the view that science is the only reliable way to acquire knowledge. Put another way, science is the only reliable road to truth. But in light of the reliability of our sense experience under standard, unhindered conditions, this claim is dubious. We obviously do know many things without the aid of scientific methodology . . .[3]

He cites love, beauty, honor, and joy (some of the most important things in life I would assert) among the intangibles that defy exact scientific analysis. He goes on to clarify the role of true science, without the dogma of scientism:

> Science may not be the only road to truth, but it is an extremely reliable way of acquiring knowledge about the empirical world. Some would say that science is reliable because it is self-correcting. Science does not grab hold of an explanation and never let go. Instead, it looks at alternative ways to explain a phenomenon, tests these alternatives, and opens up the conclusions to criticism from scientists everywhere.[3]

If you are worried about any apparent conflict between science and religion, just relax. Because at some point in the future you're going to learn that some of the things you thought you knew and understood clearly in science were really not quite right . . . and that some of the things you thought you understood in religion were not quite right either.

Both science and religion share the same goal: reveal truth. Ultimately, the two fields of knowledge will blend together smoothly like a fresh peach milkshake and will be just as sweet to the taste.

History and today's newscasts are replete with examples where the dogma trap has captured the unwary. The consequences range from the relatively benign to the down-right tragic. Let me offer up just a few more examples for your consideration. Here are a few assertions which have been treated by some as dogma, and I invite you to contemplate the consequences of dogma for yourself:

- "the black race is inferior and are natural slaves"
- "the Bible story of the Creation took exactly six 24-hour days"
- "eugenics is a true science, and its principles demand that the strong remove the weak human races from the gene pool"
- "Allah will greatly reward the faithful Muslim who takes the lives of infidels"
- "to be a true Christian one must believe the Nicene Creed, so Mormons are not Christians"
- "social engineering justifies murdering millions of your citizens"
- "only carbon-based life is possible"
- "wealth concentrated in the few will trickle down to the many"
- "David Koresh speaks for God"
- "God no longer speaks through prophets"

We have seen that being dogmatic can be an impediment to seeking truth. And we've seen that being dogmatic can lead to truly evil outcomes on occasion. But there is one, last practical point about avoiding dogma which relates to our own personal well-being and happiness. Specifically, dogma can ruin your life. How many friendships have been damaged or destroyed, how many family ties have been broken, how many unhappy lives have been lived because a person would not open their mind or their heart to someone else's idea or opinion? The Lord has admonished his people to harbor "temperance, patience, brotherly kindness, godliness, charity, humility, diligence." And he adds, "Ask, and ye shall receive; knock, and it shall be opened unto you." (D&C 4:6,7) Surely we are kind, charitable, and humble when we are willing to listen to another's sincerely held idea or belief. And how can we ask and receive if we already know the answer?

Dogmatic thinking is a trap. By contrast, I imagine we share in our admiration of Joseph Smith. It was Joseph's willingness to think outside the box and to accept and implement the unorthodox; it was his humble background and his teachable attitude that permitted him to accomplish so much in such a short lifetime. Of course, he didn't abandon all reason and good judgment, and neither should we. But let's not require a wedge and hammer to pound fresh ideas into our heads as he bemoaned, but instead let's follow his example and be open and creative in our thinking, amenable to what the Lord has to offer us, avoiding unyielding dogma. As Brother Joseph stated: "If there is anything virtuous, lovely, or of good report or praiseworthy, we seek after these things." (Article of Faith 13)

NOTES

1. Stephen F. Mason, *A History of the Sciences*, Macmillan General Reference, 1962, pp. 160–161.
2. Joseph Fielding Smith, *Teachings of the Prophet Joseph Smith*, Deseret Book, 1973, p. 331.
3. Lewis Vaughn, *The Power of Critical Thinking*, Oxford University Press, 2007, p. 386.

Chapter 14

DISCERNING BETWEEN TRUTH AND ERROR

How much better is it to get wisdom than gold! and to get understanding rather to be chosen than silver! (Proverbs 16:16)

We live in a day when it is often difficult to know what to think about almost anything. We are bombarded constantly with conflicting claims and opinions in science, religion, politics, and even questions like the advisability of eating butter. This state of affairs has come about quite recently due to three important developments over the last one hundred years or so. First is the proliferation of mass media in the form of print, radio, and TV, and the corresponding effort to reduce every complex topic into a short sound bite. Second is the recent rise of social media, which gives every person on earth equal access to the public marketplace of ideas; and therefore, the opinion of every person, whether informed or otherwise, is afforded equal air time. Both these developments are important, but fairly neutral in character in the sense that they may be used equally well for good or ill. But the third is more sinister. It is the rise of a class of professional disinformation specialists who, for financial or political motives, set out purposely to deceive and confuse, using the tools listed in the first two developments, media and social media. The apostle Paul predicted that in the last days, "evil men and seducers shall wax worse and worse, deceiving, and being deceived" (2 Timothy 3:13). As we seek truth in our own lives, how can we avoid being trapped by these kinds of deception?

Of course, there is nothing new about the scam artist and deceiver. In the nineteenth century, P. T. Barnum supposedly summed up the philosophy of this group with this famous saying, "There is a sucker born every minute." But it is ironic that there is some doubt that these were his words at all—perhaps another example of twentieth-century misinformation. Each deceiver has his or her particular motivation. Often it is money, and the patent medicine craze of the nineteenth century is an example of this phenomenon in its infancy.

In Brockville, the small town in eastern Canada where I grew up, the richest home in the richest neighborhood on the Saint Lawrence River is the Fulford mansion. This is now a museum, but in its day it was occupied by the Fulford family, who made their fortune manufacturing and selling Dr. Williams's Pink Pills for Pale People. Yes, seriously, that was the name. These pills promised cures for Saint Vitus' Dance, paralysis, neuralgia, rheumatism, headache, the after-effects of the flu, heart palpitation, pale complexions, and all forms of weakness in male or female. They were promoted with appropriate testimonials from happy customers. They were sold widely in eighty-two countries, including the United States and those of the British empire. They consisted mainly of inert materials as well as some essential minerals found in many foods. And in this respect they were no different than hundreds of other patent medicines of the day.

There was nothing particularly sinister about the pink pill business. Medical and biological sciences weren't advanced enough to explain why they should or shouldn't work; the pills were harmless, and effective outcomes were probably due to the so-called *placebo effect*. This well documented effect results from the administration of a *placebo*, often a sugar pill, to a patient who may think it is real medicine and whose physiology may be boosted into generating its own cure or health benefit simply on the basis of believing in the power of the "medicine." There apparently is real power just in believing.

The problem with many of these *medicines* was not that they did actual physical harm in most cases, but rather that they preyed on vulnerable people for financial gain by making exaggerated unproven curative claims. Beyond this, however, in other cases there were unscrupulous promoters marketing drugs and food additives that were clearly dangerous and harmful. This issue was one factor leading to the creation of the US Food and Drug Administration in the early part of the twentieth century.

As we consider traditional examples of deceivers and their motivations, a good candidate is Korihor in the Book of Mormon. He set out to convince believers that their trust in scripture and prophets was ill-founded, that there was no God, that their belief in Christ was foolishness. While Korihor's motivation was partly money—*priestcraft* the scriptures call it—it was also pride, in that it gave him an inflated sense of personal importance so that he could brag that he knew better than those fools who fell for religion. He wanted a following, a group over whom he could exert power, which in turn would feed his pride further. In the end, he came to admit that he had purposely set out to deceive, and he suffered a bitter end.

These examples of deception, and endless others like them, predate the modern world of rapid, instantaneous, and far-reaching communications. In our highly industrialized society, not only are our medicines, cars, and cell-phones mass produced, so is our information. Thus, the potential for abuse, for deception on a massive scale, both in terms of the number of people affected and the degree to which they are influenced, has risen by orders of magnitude. Furthermore, those old human motivations for deception are as alive and well as ever: money, pride, and power. And so, a whole industry has developed around this concept. Let's look at a recent science-related example.

Today, it is widely agreed among scientists, medical doctors, and everyday folks, that smoking is harmful to one's health. The ill effects of smoking had been noticed for centuries: yellow teeth, bad breath, coughing, and so on. And of course, women with their "delicate constitutions" were not to partake. As latter-day revelation unfolded through Joseph Smith, smoking was prohibited by the Lord in the Word of Wisdom. But the world in general was willing to put up with the downsides of smoking because it was cool, and besides (understood but not admitted openly) it was addictive! So the tobacco industry prospered, and tobacco was a huge money maker for many.

But . . . could smoking actually kill you? If so, that news would definitely not be good for business. Indeed, if this idea were to be established and made known widely, it would be crossing a red line that the tobacco industry was not going to allow without a fight. So the new technologies of mass communications were called upon in a revolutionary and devastating way to aid their case. Indeed, it is in this example that we see the difference between industrial scale misinformation of the last hundred years versus what went before.

By the early 1950s, scientists in the US were convinced based on several peer-reviewed independent studies that smoking can cause cancer and death. So, the tobacco industry as a group decided to hire a public relations firm to challenge the scientific evidence. Their job was to undermine public confidence in the scientists' claims. The approach, as described in the book *Merchants of Doubt*, was to "convince the public that there was 'no sound scientific basis for the charges,' and that recent reports were simply 'sensational accusations' made by publicity seeking scientists hoping to attract more funds for their research." [1] You may recognize that this fallacious argument continues to be trotted out today to undermine scientific claims of various sorts. In the tobacco case, one of the most effective ways to undermine the well-established scientific findings was to portray the scientific community as divided on the question, by seeking out a small minority of scientists who disagreed (as is their right) or, worse, by paying unscrupulous scientists to testify on behalf of the industry. The tactic was to present the industry side of the argument as being on the same level of credibility as the independent scientific side, as equally weighted, so that the public would be under the impression that neither side of the argument carried more weight than the other. And to quote Robert Park, author of the fascinating book *Voodoo Science*, "There is, alas, no scientific claim so preposterous that a scientist cannot be found to vouch for it." [2]

Another tactic in the tobacco war was to spread the word that more work needed to be done before the conclusions against tobacco could be verified; questions remained that needed to be answered. And while it is true that there can always be more work done on any scientific question, the clear majority of the scientific community had concluded that plenty of evidence existed, enough to justify the conclusion that smoking causes cancer and death. In a nutshell, the industry strategized that if they could create enough confusion in the minds of the public, and especially in the minds of legislators, they could delay almost indefinitely any loss of sales and revenue.

Those of us who are old enough remember seeing ads in popular magazines in the 1950s and '60s in which tobacco companies portrayed MDs (or their Hollywood surrogates) smoking and touting the health benefits of cigarettes. And it worked! At least for a while. The public was convinced to be skeptical of the scientific claims, and the number of smokers expanded. The astonishing thing is that by the mid-1960s, the industry's own scientists had concluded that smoking not only caused cancer but was addictive. Yet, the industry kept this quiet and continued to insist that there was no link between smoking and cancer, and no case for addiction. It was not until 2004 (forty years later!) that the industry was finally made to admit the truth and were held accountable when they were found guilty of racketeering in US federal court. Today, the World Health Organization recognizes that smoking is the known cause of or contributor to twenty-five different diseases and is responsible for five million deaths worldwide annually. How many lives could have been saved if the truth had not been purposefully obfuscated for so long and so effectively by a deceptive mass media campaign? How insightful Joseph Smith was to remove this deadly poison from the Saints' way of life long before these facts were known.

The tobacco story serves as one of the first industrial scale public relations programs to misinform and confuse the public at large about science-related issues by manipulating mass media. But what about religious issues?

Misinformation about religion has been called upon from time immemorial to justify persecution and religious strife. Consider the ancient Romans persecuting and killing Christians as supposed enemies of the state for being unwilling to worship the emperor, or medieval Christians persecuting and killing witches for supposedly causing plagues, or the Nazis persecuting and killing Jews for supposedly promoting communism and polluting the gene pool; or modern-day extremists who accuse all Muslims of being terrorists. Indeed, Latter-day Saints have endured their own persecution based on largely false or distorted information from the very earliest days of the Church. Within Joseph Smith's lifetime, three important anti-Mormon publications were responsible for much of the animosity against the Church.

The first book to be published vilifying the restored Church was *Mormonism Unveiled*, written by E. D. Howe, a non-LDS newspaper man, based on material he collected from two disaffected former members, Doctor Philastus Hurlbut (Doctor was his first given name, not his title—easiest way to get a diploma ever!) and Ezra Booth. Hurlbut had been excommunicated on grounds of immorality, while Booth was disaffected because of a perceived shortage of miracles. This book, published just four years after the founding of the Church, attempted to undercut Joseph Smith's movement largely by smearing the character of Joseph based on gossip. Its further assertion that the Book of Mormon was based on a novel written by Solomon Spaulding was given the lie when Spaulding's manuscript was found to have virtually no commonality to the Book of Mormon. Yet many people in the neighborhood of Kirtland, Ohio, where the Church was based at the time, read the book and were persuaded by it, unaware of its lack of basis in truth. The ultimate demise of the Church in that area just a few years later can in part be attributed to this publication.

Another influential anti-Mormon book appeared toward the end of Joseph Smith's life, this time in Nauvoo, Illinois. The book, *History of the Saints: Or, An Exposé of Joe Smith and Mormonism*, was written by John C. Bennett, a former counselor to Joseph who was excommunicated for immoral behavior. Its many falsehoods and distortions were again influential on the local scene among non-members and disaffected members. Along with the steady drum beat of anti-Mormon propaganda spread by a local newspaper, the *Warsaw Signal*, edited by Thomas Sharp, this book made members of the Church, and Joseph in particular, out to be monsters bent on upending the good norms of American society and taking over the state, if not the nation, in a holy war. This propaganda was a major contributor to the eventual assassination of Joseph, resulting in a great loss to the Saints and to mankind as a whole.

In our modern day, the advent of mass media and social media has been a mixed blessing and a challenge to the restored Church and to science as well. Just as you can today find every possible contradictory opinion asserted and defended about global warming, UFOs, and the benefits of fluoridated toothpaste, by the same token you can find on the internet ardent testimonials and arguments for and against the truthfulness of the Book of Mormon, the authority of modern prophets, the validity and meaning of temple rites, and every possible gospel topic. Since every opinion and claim is presented unfiltered by careful review and presented as if every opinion merited equal consideration, a person is left dazed and confused.

The apostle Paul foresaw the pitfalls that await those who seek the truth in the latter days when he admonished:

> That we henceforth be no more children, tossed to and fro, and carried about with every wind of doctrine, by the sleight of men,

and cunning craftiness, whereby they lie in wait to deceive. (Ephesians 4:14).

This challenge has never been greater than today. Clearly what we need goes well beyond the availability of information. What we need is the wisdom to filter through the information and arguments presented to us to uncover the real truth, to find true understanding. What to do?

Specifically, what steps can we take for ourselves and those dear to us to see through the noise and find the truth? While there may be no simple answer to this question, there are steps a person can take, which go a long way to clearing the path to real understanding. These steps apply equally well to resolving vexing questions in both science and religion, as well as questions dealing with the overlap between the two. We have laid the foundation for these steps in topics covered in this book so far. Consider these:

1. Be teachable.

The scriptures exhort us to be teachable, which is really a subset of being humble. When faced with conflicting claims, it is a common tendency to bring our preconceptions and biases into the argument so early that we miss an opportunity to consider seriously both sides. In the extreme case, we can be dogmatic and refuse entirely to listen to both sides before making up our minds. This approach can be detrimental not only to our own quest for truth, but also to those around us.

Take for example the case of a teenager who is given an assignment to write a report on global warming for his science class. He is interested in deciding for himself whether claims that human activity that produces carbon dioxide from burning fossil fuels is significantly warming the climate. He has found conflicting arguments on the internet and turns to his dad for help in deciding what to believe. Dad says, "I read on Facebook that that's just a bunch of bologna, and that's all I need to know."

At the same time, a neighbor's daughter approaches her mom about the same assignment. Her mom says, "Let's go to the internet together and look over the data and the arguments' pros and cons and make an informed decision."

In the first case, not only is the dad side-stepping the opportunity to find the truth for himself, he is modeling this behavior for his son, the lesson being that uninformed bias is a perfectly acceptable substitute for real learning and understanding. On the contrary, no matter which side of the argument we ultimately choose, our choice is not defensible if we are stubbornly ignorant of the facts. And if, as we have discussed, learning truth is an essential part of our progression, this approach is definitely counterproductive.

In the area of religion, an open mind is also the best approach, as described in the previous chapter. Sometimes we may think we know the correct doctrine, only to find out later that we were relying on tradition, or that our interpretation was simply flawed. If we cast ourselves in the role of seekers of truth rather than knowers only, we do well by ourselves as well as those who look to us for answers.

2. Rely on those proven to be trustworthy.

One of the great challenges in making up our minds is figuring out which "facts" we believe.

In the field of science, we have a fairly reliable method for assuring reliability of facts and claims: peer review. If it's published in a peer-reviewed journal, the likelihood that the findings are fraudulent or incorrect is quite low—not zero, but low. What scientists deduce from their findings is a little more susceptible to interpretation, but my experience is that most scientists are sincere in their effort to find the truth. For the most part, you can trust that in the process of peer review, independent specialists who are keen to pick up on faults in the data or arguments have looked over the published claims carefully and given them their approval.

When considering whom to believe in science, keep in mind that no scientist is an expert in every field. As time passes, the amount of learning in any given area of chemistry, physics, or biology expands exponentially, and the range of expertise of any given scientist gradually narrows relative to the whole. So just because someone has a PhD after their name doesn't mean they can speak authoritatively on a subject outside their specialty. As Henry Eyring, the famous Latter-day Saint chemist, said:

All men, especially those that are very able, are so often right in their dealings with people in their specialty that they forget that some other things are not their specialty and that . . . other people may have something to tell them.[3]

Where scientists seem to disagree on a scientific topic, we can look for areas of general agreement. If 90 percent plus of many scientists are making the same claim, your safest bet is to trust their judgment. There always have been and there always will be scientist dissenters to almost any scientific claim, some genuine and some with ulterior motives, but if you are not an expert yourself, you are safest siding with the majority. You might well ask, "Isn't it possible that the majority are incorrect?" Of course that's a possibility. But that's not really the right question to ask. Anything is possible. It is possible that UFOs are real, and that Elvis is really alive and living on Mars. But the salient question is, "Is it probable?" And it is unlikely (although not impossible as we have seen) that a majority of peer-reviewed scientists will be wrong on a scientific question, especially if the question has been addressed by a large number of independent scientific groups.

In religion, we don't evaluate claims by peer review, but there are authoritative figures we can turn to when questions arise. These are living prophets. Of course, there have been dissenters from the mainstream restored Church in the past and present, even at the highest ecclesiastical levels. But the vast majority of those whom we regard with the calling of prophets, seers, and revelators have followed the path of the current majority faith, and for good reasons. After Joseph Smith's death, Sidney Rigdon attempted to create an alternative congregation, as did some of the Smith family and others, but the clear majority of the modern followers of the restored gospel are found in The Church of Jesus Christ of Latter-day Saints. Why? Because therein resides the fulness of the priesthood as passed from Joseph to the twelve and their legitimate successors. When questions arise concerning topics of faith, and specifically controversial topics with conflicting views promoted on the internet or elsewhere, we can look to prophets and their writings in scripture first and foremost for reliable answers.

3. Look for tell-tale signs.

There is often a distinct difference in tone (in religion, we would call it *spirit*) between a reliable presentation of truth on the one hand versus what we might call *propaganda* on the other. This is true for topical issues both in religion and in science. A well-laid-out rational argument is generally staid in tone, presenting the facts and resulting conclusions unemotionally. A work of propaganda is often strident in tone, spending energy in pushing its point of view rather than focusing on the facts and their reasonable interpretation. The latter works also typically devote inordinate attention to denigrating not only the opposing argument but also the character of its proponents, as was the case with the detractors of Joseph Smith. Personal (*ad hominem*) attacks are a tell-tale sign of a weak argument.

4. Focus on the big picture.

Sometimes we let ourselves get so caught up in the little details of an argument that we lose sight of the big picture. For example, detractors of the Book of Mormon like to pick out single points in the story that don't line up with our current rather fuzzy knowledge of the history and anthropology of the new world— points like the presence of horses, the use of steel bows, or DNA evidence related to native Americans. There are credible arguments made by Mormon scholars in favor of the Book of Mormon on each of these points, as published elsewhere. But in the end, the Book of Mormon needs to be evaluated in balance on the basis of its strengths overall. While we can admit that not all the apparent discrepancies between the book and the historians and scientists have been resolved, we can have faith that they will be in the future as we learn more. In the meantime, we need to consider the great strengths of the book in counterbalance: principal among these the testimony of the Spirit that it is true, but also the clear doctrines contained therein, the rise of the Church, which is built upon its foundation and blesses the lives of so many in so many ways. The great benefits derived from the book far outweigh any arguments against it based on minor points of apparent conflict with current science. We can exercise faith that any apparent conflicts will be resolved in time.

5. Look for consistency.

One of the great strengths that Joseph Smith's teachings share with science is the value they place on rational thought and the close compatibility among the various teachings. For example, as new insights into the functioning of the natural world are discovered in science, they are always evaluated in light of current understanding. If a new model or idea does not fit in with currently accepted models, this extraordinary claim is said to require extraordinary proofs, an oft-quoted saying of astrophysicist Carl Sagan.[4] The more revolutionary the claim, that is, the more it flies in the face of currently accepted science, the greater body of proof is required for the new claim to be given serious consideration. In contrast, most scientific advances simply extend current thinking into new realms and don't require rethinking currently accepted models.

For example, when the neutron was discovered in the 1930s, this added to our understanding of the functioning of the atom without having to completely rework the structure of the atom. We still thought of atoms as consisting of a positive nucleus surrounded by negative electrons. But when Einstein postulated that gravity was not a force as Newton described, but instead was a side-effect of curved four-dimensional space-time, that was an extraordinary claim that required rethinking everything that we thought we understood about the nature of space and time. Einstein's new claim required extraordinary proof and had to overcome years of skepticism by the scientific establishment. By the same token, when someone tries to sell you free energy pulled out of the air so that you never have to pay another light bill, you should look for extraordinary proof before investing. Why? Because that is an extraordinary claim that would upend all current scientific thought. You should ask: If the claim is true, what alternative scientific reality can the sellers provide to explain how their claim works? And if they can't explain it in terms understandable to the educated layman, run away!

Jesus made an extraordinary claim that he was the son of God and presented extraordinary proofs that indeed he was. He needed to provide extraordinary proofs in the form of miracles because to the Jews of his day his claim required a complete rethinking of what they thought they knew about their religion. By the same token, Joseph Smith's revolutionary claims also required extraordinary proofs in the form of the Book of Mormon and other inspired works. But as is true in science, in religion these kinds of revolutionary events come rarely, and the usual process of progress is slow and steady, involving incremental advances that are consistent with what we already think we know. Indeed, one of the reasons we have scripture is as a yardstick against which we can measure new claims in religion. It makes it possible for us to identify Korihors and recognize them for who they are.

6. Examine motivations.

Does the person making an argument stand to gain financially, politically, or in some other way from the outcome? If so, there exists a potential conflict of interest. That doesn't necessarily mean that the point of view is wrong, but it weakens the argument, and one ought to look to see if witnesses who are more independent are in agreement. The authors of the anti-Mormon books of early Church history all had grudges against Joseph Smith and stood to gain in one form or another from their publications. The promoters of cold fusion had much to gain financially if their claims held water, but even when the claims were recognized as faulty, they continued to search for financial backing for their work. Yet their belief in cold fusion placed them in a small minority among scientists generally. Rarely if ever would the entire scientific community conspire to deceive in favor of research funding. Why? Because scientific reputations are just as readily built on debunking bad ideas. And a scientist's credibility is everything—any good scientist knows not to purposely stake his credibility on a bogus claim, as it will ruin his career once the truth comes out. It certainly ruined the careers of Pons and Fleischmann.

7. "By their fruits ye shall know them."

Sometimes it takes time for the validity or error of an idea to become known. And for this reason it is often wise to avoid a rush to judgment—keeping an open mind has its rewards in the end. In the meantime, taking the safe road may well be the best course. The Word of Wisdom aside, it took a long time for scientific research to establish the details of a clear link between smoking and death. The wise course for anyone not willing to take the Lord at his word and sitting on the fence on this issue would have been to avoid smoking altogether until the jury came in. The risks of being wrong were too great. With time, the fruits of abstinence versus indulgence were made clear by careful studies. The same approach can be applied to any question, scientific or religious, where the risks of being wrong outweigh any argument to the contrary. Given time, the right choice can often become clear, and in the meantime, prudence is called for.

In the end, it is largely for each person to use his or her wits to evaluate what is true and what is not. Nevertheless, we do not need to be alone in this endeavor. In this day of confusion, those who share an added measure of the spirit of God through the gift of the Holy Ghost have a distinct advantage. But this does not mean that the Lord does not expect us to use every tool at our disposal to discern truth from error. He has given us guidelines through the scriptures and living prophets, and he has shared with us his ability to reason so that we can make wise choices if we inform ourselves through study and personal experience. No doubt we will make mistakes, yet our mortal experience is not just a proving ground but is perhaps the best teacher in our ongoing quest for truth.

NOTES

1. Naomi Oreskes and Erik M. Conway, *Merchants of Doubt*, Bloomsbury Press, 2010, p. 15.
2. Robert Park, "The Seven Warning Signs of Bogus Science," *The Chronicle of Higher Education*, January 31, 2003.
3. Henry J. Eyring, *Mormon Scientist*, Deseret Book, 2007, p. 297.
4. Carl Sagan, *Cosmos*, Digitally Remastered Disc Collector's Edition, Cosmos Studios Inc., 2000.

Chapter 15

JOSEPH THE SEER

No man knows my history. I cannot tell it: I shall never undertake it. . . . If I had not experienced what I have, I could not have believed it myself. (Teachings of the Prophet Joseph Smith, p. 361)

In 1844, a prominent New Englander, Josiah Quincy, visited Nauvoo as part of a tour of the American frontier and spent a day with the prophet Joseph Smith just weeks before Joseph's death. Quincy later wrote a book about his various journeys, *Figures of the Past*, and said this about the man:

> It is by no means improbable that some future textbook, for the use of generations yet unborn, will contain a question something like this: What historical American of the nineteenth century has exerted the most powerful influence upon the destinies of his countrymen? And it is by no means impossible that the answer to that interrogatory may be thus written: Joseph Smith, the Mormon prophet. And the reply, absurd as it doubtless seems to most men now living, may be an obvious commonplace to their descendants. History deals in surprises and paradoxes quite as startling as this. The man who established a religion in this age of free debate, who was and is today accepted by hundreds of thousands as a direct emissary from the Most High,—such a rare human being is not to be disposed of by pelting his memory with unsavory epithets. Fanatic, imposter, charlatan, he may have been; but these hard names furnish no solution to the problem he presents to us. Fanatics and impostors are living and

dying every day, and their memory is buried with them; but the wonderful influence which this founder of a religion exerted and still exerts throws him into relief before us, not as a rogue to be criminated, but as a phenomenon to be explained. . . . If the reader does not know just what to make of Joseph Smith, I cannot help him out of the difficulty. I myself stand helpless before the puzzle.[1]

Quincy was a Harvard-educated Bostonian and later became mayor of that city. It is no wonder that he and many others like him, both then and since, have found it difficult to fathom Joseph Smith. How could Joseph at once be a simple backwoodsman and yet make such a powerful and positive contribution to the world in so many areas? And as we have considered herein, his amazing insights into the nature of the physical world, foreshadowing many aspects of natural science as yet undiscovered, we add an additional level of complexity to this conundrum. Was Joseph a genius savant who somehow intuited the true nature of things, or was he a huckster who simply shot from the hip and got lucky time and again, or was he what he claimed to be—a prophet who gained his understanding from the greatest teacher of them all?

Those who honor Joseph Smith as a prophet do so for a multitude of reasons. They have put his claims to the test by reading the Book of Mormon and seeking a spiritual witness; they have studied Joseph's other inspired writings and sermons; they have lived the principles he espoused and enjoyed their fruits. And while I know of no one who has been converted to The Church of Jesus Christ of Latter-day Saints because of Joseph's insights into natural science, these inspired insights are very much worthy of consideration. Joseph's limited allusions to scientific principles add an extra measure of testimony to the truthfulness of his other claims. In the end, one must come to judge Joseph's assertion that he was a prophet based on the totality of his contributions. His deep and anticipatory insights into nature constitute a significant contribution to the many reasons that his claims should be taken seriously. They comprise one small but important piece of the "puzzle" that Josiah Quincy found to be Joseph Smith.

We have seen how Joseph Smith's theology is a rational theology that makes it much more compatible with a scientific approach to truth than much of traditional Christian doctrine. This rational theology makes God a part of nature rather than existing outside nature, so that miracles are not intrinsically unknowable, but in fact manifest the operation of natural laws as yet not understood by man. According to Joseph, man can progress in knowledge and therefore power to become like God and manipulate nature in like ways, a progression in understanding that parallels the scientific search for truth about the natural world. His theology embraces truth from science as emanating from a Heavenly Father who wishes to endow his children with as much truth as possible for their benefit and progression. This ongoing quest for truth rejects dogmatic adherence to unproven ideas and encourages an openness to new revelation and insight from whatever reliable source.

In his revelations, Joseph anticipated the vastness of God's creations in the form of stars and inhabited worlds, the degree to which only later did science begin to uncover. His teachings concerning spirit and the existence of unseen worlds contiguous to our own defied the science of his day but are perfectly compatible with the twenty-first-century understanding of the world of matter and light. He had insight into the nature of light and its relationship to life and intelligent thought that was far in advance of the science of his day. He anticipated with greater clarity than ever the roles of opposing forces of good and evil as they relate to the forces of cosmos and chaos in nature. He resolved the age-old paradox of free will and accountability with his teaching that man is co-eternal with God; while the science of his day implied that the universe and man were mechanical in nature, and therefore that free will was an illusion, in the following century science came to understand that the universe is not mechanical, but that uncertainty is a property of nature that opens the door wide to the concept of free will. He embraced the possibility of an earth billions of years old and the concept of relative time long before Einstein enlarged on these ideas. He encouraged his Saints to seek out all that is "virtuous, lovely, or of good report or praiseworthy," and his successor Brigham Young made it clear that science is a reliable source of such things to be embraced.

As apostle John A. Widtsoe wrote:

> Certainly the claim cannot be made that Joseph Smith anticipated the world of science in the recognition of this important principle [that the world is governed by natural law]; but it is a source of marvel that he should so clearly recognize and state it, at a time when many religious sects and philosophical creeds chose to assume that natural laws could be set aside easily

by mystical methods that might be acquired by anyone. In some respects, the scientific test of the divine inspiration of Joseph Smith lies here. Ignorant and superstitious as his enemies say he was, the mystical would have attracted him greatly, and he would have played for his own interest upon the superstitious fears of his followers. Instead, he taught doctrines absolutely free from mysticism, and built a system of religion in which the invariable relation of cause and effect is the cornerstone.[2]

Many of the novel ideas that Joseph Smith taught have since that day been confirmed by science, or at least are found to be compatible with the science of our day. This is not to say, however, that unresolved questions don't remain. There are some points on which Joseph and modern science still do not seem to align. But it is important to keep in mind that two hundred years ago, there were many more such points of apparent non-alignment which in the interim have come to be resolved. This has been the principle theme of this work. In essence, the moral of the story is this: Having seen the resolution of several important points of apparent disagreement in the past, we can have faith that given time and the revealing of additional information, remaining points can and will be resolved.

It is unfortunate that we lost Joseph Smith at such an early age. Yet it is remarkable how much he was able to teach us in the short years that he lived. He once said: "God hath not revealed anything to Joseph, but what He will make known unto the Twelve, and even the least Saint may know all things as fast as he is able to bear them."[3a] But he later qualified this statement with, "Some people say I am a fallen Prophet, because I do not bring forth more of the word of the Lord. Why do I not do it? Are we able to receive it? No."[3b] And even later, "Paul saw the third heavens, and I more."[3c] Apparently our limited ability to "bear" new truths has constrained what the Lord has been willing to share. No doubt this comes about because knowledge can bring about great evil as well as great good. Indeed, mankind's ability to apply nature's secrets for creating more destructive weapons of war stands as a stark testament to this unfortunate reality. As we prepare ourselves properly, we can look forward to greater blessings of knowledge and wisdom and the fulfillment of Joseph's vision for every Saint:

If thou shalt ask, thou shalt receive revelation upon revelation, knowledge upon knowledge, that thou mayest know the mysteries and peaceable things—that which bringeth joy, that which bringeth life eternal. (D&C 42:61)

NOTES

1. Josiah Quincy, *Figures of the Past from the Leaves of Old Journals*, 3rd ed., Library of Congress, 1883, pp. 376–400.
2. John A. Widtsoe, *Joseph Smith as Scientist*, General Board Young Men's Improvement Associations,1908; reprinted by Archive Publishers, 2000, p. 18.
3. Joseph Fielding Smith, *Teachings of the Prophet Joseph Smith*, Deseret Book, 1973, *a*: p. 149, *b*: p. 194, *c*: p. 301.

About the Author

Dr. John David Lamb retired in 2014 as Eliot A. Butler Professor of Chemistry after thirty-six years at Brigham Young University. He served as editor-in-chief of a major scientific journal and as BYU Associate Dean of Undergraduate Education. He was recipient of many of BYU's top honors for teaching and research, including its highest faculty award, the Maeser Distinguished Faculty Lectureship. He was a visiting lecturer at universities in Italy, Germany, and China. He was a member of the Mormon Tabernacle Choir and chair of the LDS Priesthood Manuals Writing Committee and is a visual artist whose works have been displayed in juried art exhibits. He and his wife, Betty, have six sons and eleven grandchildren.

Scan to visit

www.johndavidlamb.com